English/Polish Edition

The New Oxford Picture Dictionary

E. C. Parnwell

Translated by Maciej Sienicki

Illustrations by:
Ray Burns
Bob Giuliani
Laura Hartman
Pamela Johnson
Melodye Rosales
Raymond Skibinski
Joel Snyder

Oxford University Press

Oxford University Press
200 Madison Avenue
New York, NY 10016 USA

Walton Street
Oxford OX2 6DP England

OXFORD is a trademark of Oxford University Press.

ISBN 0-19-434650-1

*The publishers would like to thank the following
agents for their cooperation:*

Carol Bancroft and Friends, representing Bob
Giuliani, Laura Hartman, and Melodye Rosales.

Publishers Graphics Inc., representing Ray
Burns, Pamela Johnson, and Joel Snyder.

Cover illustration by Laura Hartman.

Printed in Hong Kong.
Printing (last digit): 10 9 8 7 6 5 4 3 2

The New Oxford Picture Dictionary contextually illustrates over 2,400 words. The book is a unique language learning tool for students of English. It provides students with a glance at American lifestyle, as well as a compendium of useful vocabulary.

The *Dictionary* is organized thematically, beginning with topics that are most useful for the "survival" needs of students in an English-speaking country. However, pages may be used at random, depending on the students' particular needs. The book need not be taught in order.

The New Oxford Picture Dictionary contextualizes vocabulary whenever possible. Verbs have been included on separate pages, but within a topic area where they are most likely to occur. However, this does not imply that these verbs only appear within these contexts.

Articles are shown only with irregular nouns. Regional variations of the primary translation are listed following a slash (/). A complete index with pronunciation guide in English is in the Appendix.

For further ideas on using *The New Oxford Picture Dictionary*, see the *Teacher's Guide* and the two workbooks: *Beginner's* and *Intermediate* levels. Also available in the program are a complete set of *Cassettes*, offering a reading of all of the words in the *Dictionary; Vocabulary Playing Cards*, featuring 40 words and the corresponding pictures on 80 cards, with ideas for many games; and sets of *Wall Charts*, available in one complete package or in three smaller packages. All of these items are available in English only.

Nowy Oksfordzki Słownik Obrazkowy ilustruje 240 tysięcy słów w kontekście. Książka ta jest jedyną w swoim rodzaju pomocą dla uczących się języka angielskiego. Daje ona wgląd w amerykański styl życia i dostarcza podstawowego zasobu słów.

Słownik jest uporządkowany tematycznie, zaczynając od informacji najbardziej potrzebnych uczniowi do "przetrwania" w kraju anglojęzycznym. Poszczególnych stron można jednak używać w sposób dowolny w zależności od indywidualnych potrzeb uczniów. Nie jest konieczne przerabianie materiału w jakiejś określonej kolejności.

Gdzie tylko możliwe *Nowy Oksfordzki Słownik Obrazkowy* podaje słowa w kontekście, w którym są one używane. Czasowniki są podane na osobnych stronach, ale w obrębie tematyki, w której najczęściej się ich używa. Nie oznacza to jednak, że są to jedyne konteksty, w jakich czasowniki te występują.

Przedimki są podane wyłącznie z rzeczownikami nieregularnymi. Warianty regionalne podstawowego tłumaczenia są zaznaczone ukośną kreską(/). Kompletny indeks wraz z opisem reguł wymowy po angielsku umieszczony jest w Aneksie.

Pewne sugestie co do wykorzystania *Nowego Oksfordzkiego Słownika Obrazkowego* można znaleźć w przewodniku dla nauczyciela (*Teacher's Guide*) i dwóch książkach ćwiczeń: dla początkujących (*Beginner's Workbook*) i średniozaawansowanych (*Intermediate Workbook*).

Dostępne są również: pełen zestaw kaset z nagraniem wszystkich wyrazów występujących w *Słowniku*, foliogramy, oraz zestawy plansz na ścianę, które można kupić w jednym pełnym zestawie, lub w trzech osobnych pakietach. Wszystkie te materiały są dostępne tylko w języku angielskim.

Spis treści

		Page
People and Relationships	Ludzie i pokrewieństwa	2
The Family	Rodzina	3
The Human Body	Ciało człowieka	4–5
Vegetables	Warzywa	6–7
Fruits	Owoce	8–9
Meat, Poultry, and Seafood	Mięso, drób i owoce morza	10–11
Containers, Quantities, and Money	Pojemniki, ilości i pieniądze	12–13
The Supermarket	Supermarket	14–15
Family Restaurant and Cocktail Lounge	Restauracja rodzinna i bar koktailowy	16
Restaurant Verbs	Czasowniki związane z restauracją	17
Common Prepared Foods	Popularne dania	18
Outdoor Clothes	Ubrania wierzchnie	19
Everyday Clothes	Ubrania na co dzień	20–21
Underwear and Sleepwear	Bielizna dzienna i nocna	22
Jewelry and Cosmetics	Biżuteria i kosmetyki	23
Describing Clothes	Opis ubrania	24
Describing the Weather	Opis pogody	25
Seasonal Verbs	Czasowniki związane z porami roku	26
Houses	Domy	27
The Living Room	Pokój dzienny	28
The Dining Room	Jadalnia	29
The Kitchen	Kuchnia	30
Kitchen Verbs	Czasowniki związane z kuchnią	31
The Bedroom	Sypialnia	32
The Baby's Room	Pokój dziecięcy	33
The Bathroom	Łazienka	34
The Utility Room	Pokój gospodarczy	35
A Workshop	Warsztat	36–37
Housework and Repair Verbs	Czasowniki dotyczące prac domowych i naprawą	38
Medical and Dental Care	Opieka medyczna i dentystyczna	39
Ailments and Injuries	Dolegliwości i urazy	40
Treatments and Remedies	Leczenie i leki	41
Firefighting and Rescue	Pożarnictwo i ratownictwo	42
Crime and Punishment	Przestępstwo i kara	43
The City	Miasto	44–45
The U.S. Postal System	Poczta w Stanach Zjednoczonych	46
The Public Library	Biblioteka publiczna	47
The Armed Forces	Siły zbrojne	48
Trucks	Ciężarówki	49
Cars	Samochody osobowe	50–51
Bikes	Rowery	52
Highway Travel	Podróż drogą	53
Public Transportation	Komunikacja	54–55
Air Travel	Podróż lotnicza	56
Aircraft	Statki powietrzne	57
In Port	W porcie	58
Pleasure Boating	Sporty wodne	59
Plants and Trees	Rośliny i drzewa	60–61
Simple Animals	Zwierzęta proste	62
Insects	Owady	63

Page

Birds   Ptaki   64

Fish and Reptiles   Ryby i gady   65

Mammals I   Ssaki I   66–67

Mammals II   Ssaki II   68–69

Map of the World   Mapa świata   70–71

The United States of America   Stany Zjednoczone Ameryki   72–73

The Universe   Wszechświat   74

The Space Program   Program kosmiczny   75

The Classroom   Klasa, sala szkolna   76

School Verbs   Czasowniki związane ze szkołą   77

A Science Lab   Laboratorium fizyczno-chemiczne   78

Math   Matematyka   79

Energy   Energia   80

Farming and Ranching   Rolnictwo i hodowla   81

Construction   Budownictwo   82

An Office   Biuro   83

Occupations I: Main Street USA   Zawody I: przy głównej ulicy w USA   84

Occupations II   Zawody II   85

Occupations III   Zawody III   86

Neighborhood Parks   Park osiedlowy   87

Outdoor Activities   Zajęcia na świeżym powietrzu   88–89

At the Beach   Na plaży   90–91

Team Sports   Gry zespołowe   92

Ballfields   Boiska do gry w piłkę   93

Individual Sports   Sporty indywidualne   94

Fields and Courses   Boiska i tereny sportowe   95

Sports Verbs   Czasowniki związane ze sportem   96–97

Musical Instruments   Instrumenty muzyczne   98

Music, Dance, and Theater   Muzyka, taniec i teatr   99

Electronics and Photography   Elektronika i fotografia   100

Handicrafts   Prace ręczne   101

Prepositions of Description   Przyimki opisowe   102

Prepositions of Motion   Przyimki ruchu   103

Appendix   Aneks   104

Index   Indeks   105

kobieta	**1.** woman		dzieci	**7.** children
mężczyzna	**2.** man		chłopiec	**8.** boy
mąż	**3.** husband		dziewczynka	**9.** girl
żona	**4.** wife		dziadkowie	**10.** grandparents
dziecko	**5.** baby		wnuczka	**11.** granddaughter
rodzice	**6.** parents		wnuczek	**12.** grandson

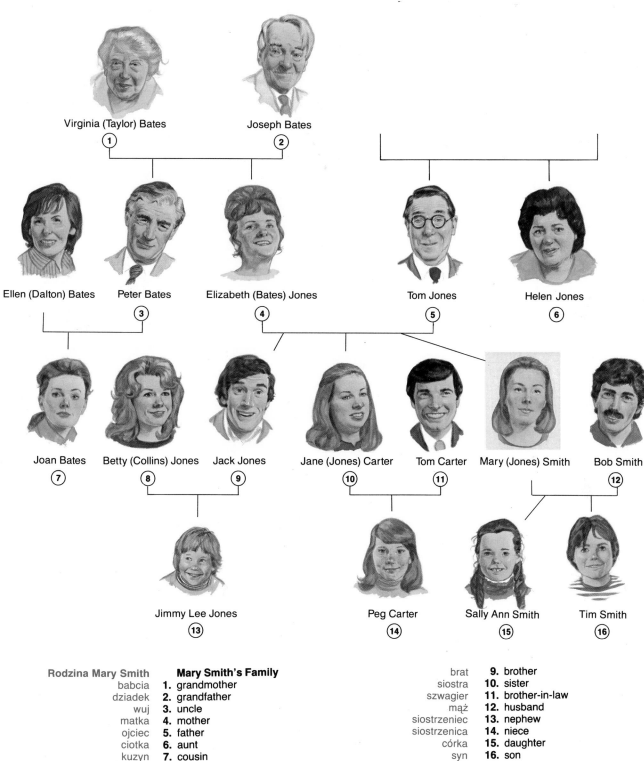

Virginia (Taylor) Bates ①   Joseph Bates ②

Ellen (Dalton) Bates   Peter Bates ③   Elizabeth (Bates) Jones ④   Tom Jones ⑤   Helen Jones ⑥

Joan Bates ⑦   Betty (Collins) Jones ⑧   Jack Jones ⑨   Jane (Jones) Carter ⑩   Tom Carter ⑪   Mary (Jones) Smith   Bob Smith ⑫

Jimmy Lee Jones ⑬   Peg Carter ⑭   Sally Ann Smith ⑮   Tim Smith ⑯

Rodzina Mary Smith		Mary Smith's Family		
babcia	**1.** grandmother	brat	**9.** brother
dziadek	**2.** grandfather	siostra	**10.** sister
wuj	**3.** uncle	szwagier	**11.** brother-in-law
matka	**4.** mother	mąż	**12.** husband
ojciec	**5.** father	siostrzeniec	**13.** nephew
ciotka	**6.** aunt	siostrzenica	**14.** niece
kuzyn	**7.** cousin	córka	**15.** daughter
szwagierka	**8.** sister-in-law	syn	**16.** son

A

B

C

D

Ciało	A. The Body
twarz	**1.** face
usta	**2.** mouth
podbródek	**3.** chin
szyja	**4.** neck
bark	**5.** shoulder
ramię, ręka	**6.** arm
ramię	**7.** upper arm
łokieć	**8.** elbow
przedramię	**9.** forearm
pacha	**10.** armpit
plecy	**11.** back
pierś	**12.** chest
pas	**13.** waist
brzuch	**14.** abdomen
pośladki	**15.** buttocks
biodro	**16.** hip
noga	**17.** leg
udo	**18.** thigh
kolano	**19.** knee
łydka	**20.** calf

Ręka	B. The Hand
przegub	**21.** wrist
knykieć	**22.** knuckle

paznokieć	**23.** fingernail
kciuk	**24.** thumb
palec wskazujący	**25.** (index) finger
palec środkowy	**26.** middle finger
palec serdeczny	**27.** ring finger
palec mały	**28.** little finger
dłoń	**29.** palm

Głowa	C. The Head
włosy	**30.** hair
przedziałek	**31.** part
czoło	**32.** forehead
bak	**33.** sideburn
ucho	**34.** ear
policzek	**35.** cheek
nos	**36.** nose
nozdrze	**37.** nostril
szczęka	**38.** jaw
broda	**39.** beard
wąsy	**40.** mustache
język	**41.** tongue
ząb	**42.** tooth
warga	**43.** lip

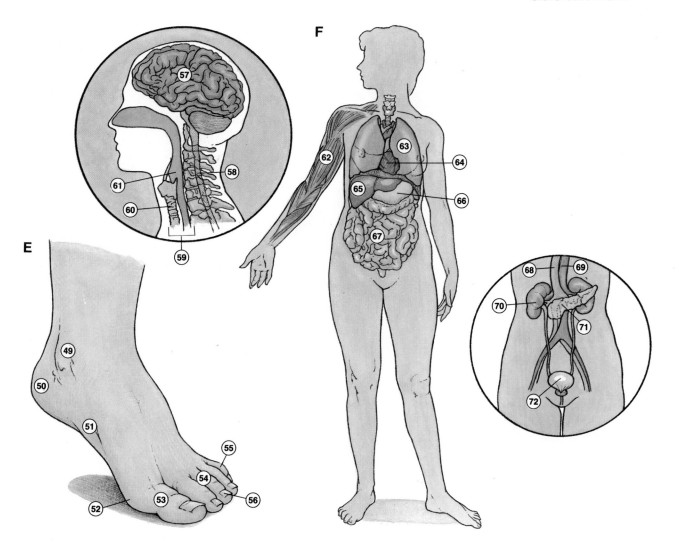

Oko	**D. The Eye**
brew	**44.** eyebrow
powieka	**45.** eyelid
rzęsy	**46.** eyelashes
tęczówka	**47.** iris
źrenica	**48.** pupil

Stopa	**E. The Foot**
kostka	**49.** ankle
pięta	**50.** heel
podbicie	**51.** instep
kostka	**52.** ball
duży palec	**53.** big toe
palec u nogi	**54.** toe
mały palec	**55.** little toe
paznokieć	**56.** toenail

Narządy wewnętrzne	**F. The Internal Organs**
mózg	**57.** brain
rdzeń kręgowy	**58.** spinal cord
gardło	**59.** throat
tchawica	**60.** windpipe
przełyk	**61.** esophagus
mięsień	**62.** muscle
płuco	**63.** lung
serce	**64.** heart
wątroba	**65.** liver
żołądek	**66.** stomach
jelita	**67.** intestines
żyła	**68.** vein
tętnica	**69.** artery
nerka	**70.** kidney
trzustka	**71.** pancreas
pęcherz	**72.** bladder

kalafior	**1.** (head of) cauliflower
brokuły	**2.** broccoli
kapusta	**3.** cabbage
brukselka	**4.** brussels sprouts
rzeżucha	**5.** watercress
sałata zielona	**6.** lettuce
cykoria	**7.** escarole
szpinak	**8.** spinach
zioło (ła)	**9.** herb(s)
seler naciowy	**10.** celery

karczoch	**11.** artichoke
kukurydza (kaczan)	**12.** (ear of) corn
kolba	**a.** cob
fasola	**13.** kidney bean(s)
fasola czarna	**14.** black bean(s)
fasolka szparagowa	**15.** string bean(s)
jaś	**16.** lima bean(s)
zielony groszek	**17.** pea(s)
strąk	**a.** pod
szparagi	**18.** asparagus

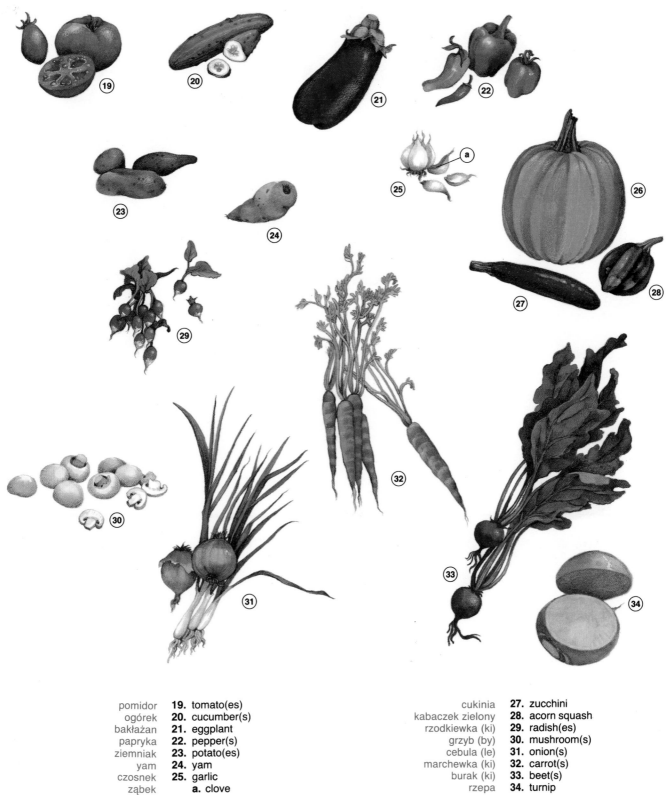

pomidor	**19.** tomato(es)		cukinia	**27.** zucchini
ogórek	**20.** cucumber(s)		kabaczek zielony	**28.** acorn squash
bakłażan	**21.** eggplant		rzodkiewka (ki)	**29.** radish(es)
papryka	**22.** pepper(s)		grzyb (by)	**30.** mushroom(s)
ziemniak	**23.** potato(es)		cebula (le)	**31.** onion(s)
yam	**24.** yam		marchewka (ki)	**32.** carrot(s)
czosnek	**25.** garlic		burak (ki)	**33.** beet(s)
ząbek	**a.** clove		rzepa	**34.** turnip
dynia	**26.** pumpkin			

(kiść) winogron	**1.**	(a bunch of) grapes
jabłko	**2.**	apple
ogonek		**a.** stem
gniazdo nasienne		**b.** core
kokos	**3.**	coconut
ananas	**4.**	pineapple
mango	**5.**	mango
melonowiec	**6.**	papaya
Owoce cytrusowe		**Citrus Fruits**
grapefruit	**7.**	grapefruit
pomarańcza	**8.**	orange
cząstka		**a.** section
skórka		**b.** rind
pestka		**c.** seed

cytryna	**9.**	lemon
limona	**10.**	lime
Owoce jagodowe		**Berries**
agrest	**11.**	gooseberries
jeżyna	**12.**	blackberries
żurawina	**13.**	cranberries
czarna jagoda	**14.**	blueberries
truskawka	**15.**	strawberry
malina	**16.**	raspberries
nektarynka	**17.**	nectarine
gruszka	**18.**	pear

wiśnia	**19.** cherries		**Orzechy**	**Nuts**
(kiść) bananów	**20.** (a bunch of) bananas		nerkowiec	**27.** cashew(s)
skórka	**a.** peel		orzeszek (ki) ziemny (ne)	**28.** peanut(s)
			orzech (chy) włoski (kie)	**29.** walnut(s)
			orzech (chy) laskowy (we)	**30.** hazelnut(s)
Suszone owoce	**Dried Fruits**		migdał (ły)	**31.** almond(s)
figa	**21.** fig		kasztan (ny)	**32.** chestnut(s)
śliwka	**22.** prune			
daktyl	**23.** date		awokado	**33.** avocado
rodzynek	**24.** raisin(s)		śliwka	**34.** plum
			melon wonny	**35.** honeydew melon
morela	**25.** apricot		kantalupa	**36.** cantaloupe
arbuz	**26.** watermelon		brzoskwinia	**37.** peach
			pestka	**a.** pit
			skórka	**b.** skin

A

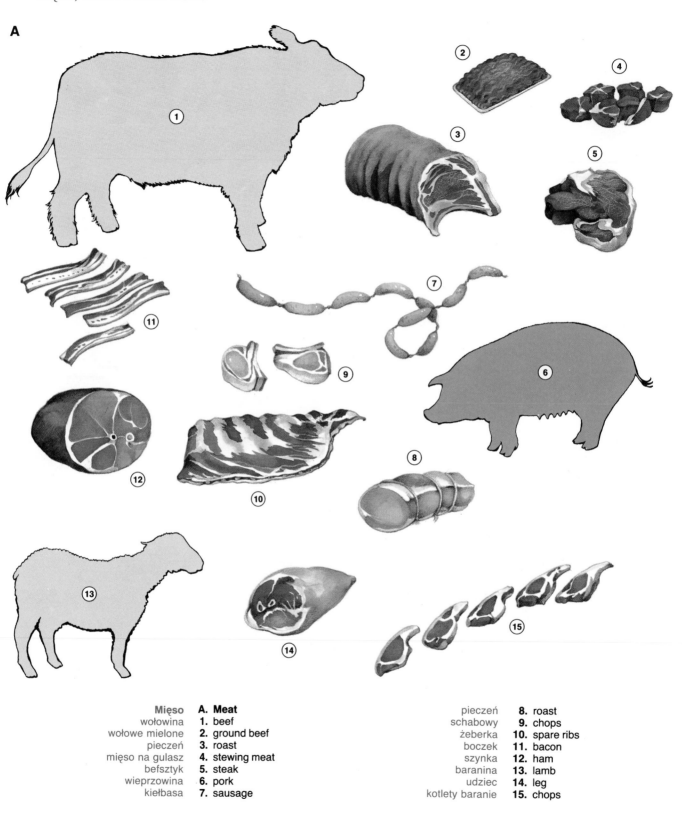

Mięso	A. Meat		pieczeń	8. roast
wołowina	1. beef		schabowy	9. chops
wołowe mielone	2. ground beef		żeberka	10. spare ribs
pieczeń	3. roast		boczek	11. bacon
mięso na gulasz	4. stewing meat		szynka	12. ham
befsztyk	5. steak		baranina	13. lamb
wieprzowina	6. pork		udziec	14. leg
kiełbasa	7. sausage		kotlety baranie	15. chops

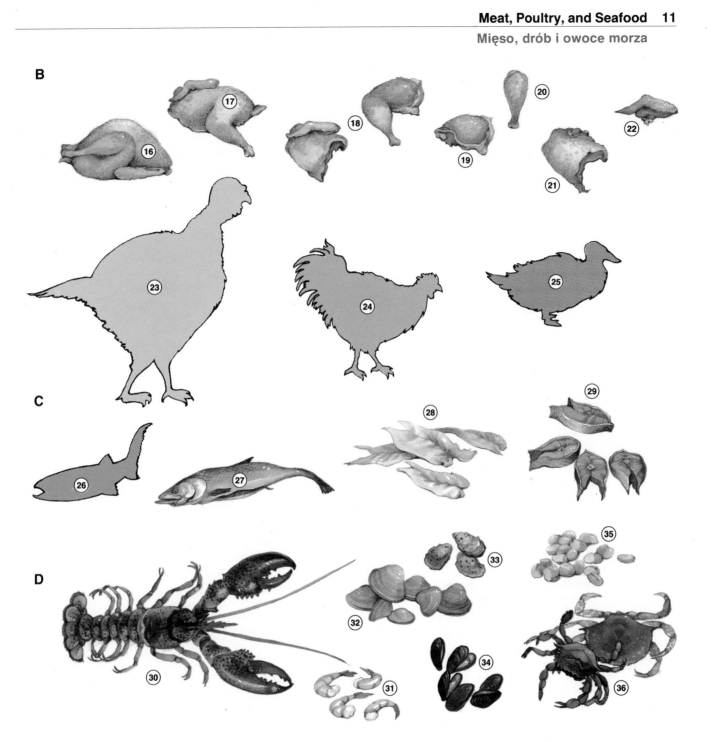

Drób	**B. Poultry**
kurczak (cały)	**16.** whole (chicken)
połówka kurczaka	**17.** split
ćwiartka	**18.** quarter
udko	**19.** thigh
noga	**20.** leg
pierś	**21.** breast
skrzydełko	**22.** wing
indyk	**23.** turkey
kurczak	**24.** chicken
kaczka	**25.** duck

Owoce morza	**C. Seafood**
ryba	**26.** fish

cała	**27.** whole
filet	**28.** filet
dzwonko	**29.** steak

Mięczaki i skorupiaki	**D. Shellfish**
homar	**30.** lobster
krewetka	**31.** shrimp
małż (że)	**32.** clam(s)
ostryga (gi)	**33.** oyster(s)
mula (le)	**34.** mussel(s)
mięso przegrzebka	**35.** scallop(s)
krab (by)	**36.** crab(s)

Pojemniki, ilości i pieniądze

karton	**1.** carton	bochenek	**7.** loaf
pojemnik	**2.** container	torebka	**8.** bag
butelka	**3.** bottle	słoik	**9.** jar
opakowanie	**4.** package	puszka	**10.** can
paczka	**5.** stick	rolka	**11.** roll
kubełek	**6.** tub		

pudełko	**12.** box
zestaw sześciu puszek	**13.** six-pack
dozownik	**14.** pump
tuba	**15.** tube
paczka	**16.** pack
książeczka	**17.** book
tabliczka, porcja, kawałek	**18.** bar
filiżanka	**19.** cup
szklanka	**20.** glass
kromka, plasterek, kawałek	**21.** slice
kawałek	**22.** piece

| miska, głęboki talerz | **23.** bowl |
| pojemnik z aerozolem | **24.** spray can |

Pieniądze	**Money**
banknoty dolarowe	**25.** dollar bills
monety	**26.** coins
cent	**27.** penny
pięć centów	**28.** nickel
dziesięć centów	**29.** dime
dwadzieścia pięć centów	**30.** quarter

Supermarket

dział delikatesowy	**1.** deli counter		koszyk	**8.** shopping basket
mrożonki	**2.** frozen foods		płody rolne	**9.** produce
zamrażarka	**3.** freezer		przejście	**10.** aisle
produkty nabiałowe	**4.** dairy products		wypieki	**11.** baked goods
mleko	**5.** milk		chleb	**12.** bread
półka	**6.** shelf		produkty w puszkach	**13.** canned goods
waga	**7.** scale		napoje	**14.** beverages

FISH MEAT POULTRY

przedmioty gospodarstwa domowego	**15.** household items	kasjer	**22.** cashier
lada chłodnicza	**16.** bin	taśma	**23.** conveyor belt
klient	**17.** customer	produkty spożywcze	**24.** groceries
przekąski	**18.** snacks	torba	**25.** bag
wózek	**19.** shopping cart	stanowisko kasowe	**26.** checkout counter
paragon	**20.** receipt	czek	**27.** check
kasa	**21.** cash register		

Restauracja rodzinna i bar koktailowy

Restauracja rodzinna	**A. Family Restaurant**	Bar koktailowy	**B. Cocktail Lounge**
kucharz	**1.** cook	korkociąg	**17.** corkscrew
kelnerka	**2.** waitress	korek	**18.** cork
pomocnik	**3.** busboy	wino	**19.** wine
keczup	**4.** ketchup	kran	**20.** tap
kelner	**5.** waiter	barman	**21.** bartender
fartuch	**6.** apron	napój alkoholowy (butelka)	**22.** liquor (bottle)
karta dań	**7.** menu	piwo	**23.** beer
wysokie krzesło	**8.** high chair	bar	**24.** bar
odgrodzenie	**9.** booth	stołek barowy	**25.** bar stool
słomka	**10.** straw	fajka	**26.** pipe
napój orzeźwiający	**11.** soft drink	podstawki	**27.** coaster
szafa grająca	**12.** jukebox	zapałki (w książeczce)	**28.** (book of) matches
cukier (w torebce)	**13.** sugar (packet)	popielniczka	**29.** ashtray
rachunek	**14.** check	zapalniczka	**30.** lighter
herbata	**15.** tea	papieros	**31.** cigarette
kanapka	**16.** sandwich	kelnerka roznosząca koktaile	**32.** cocktail waitress
		taca	**33.** tray

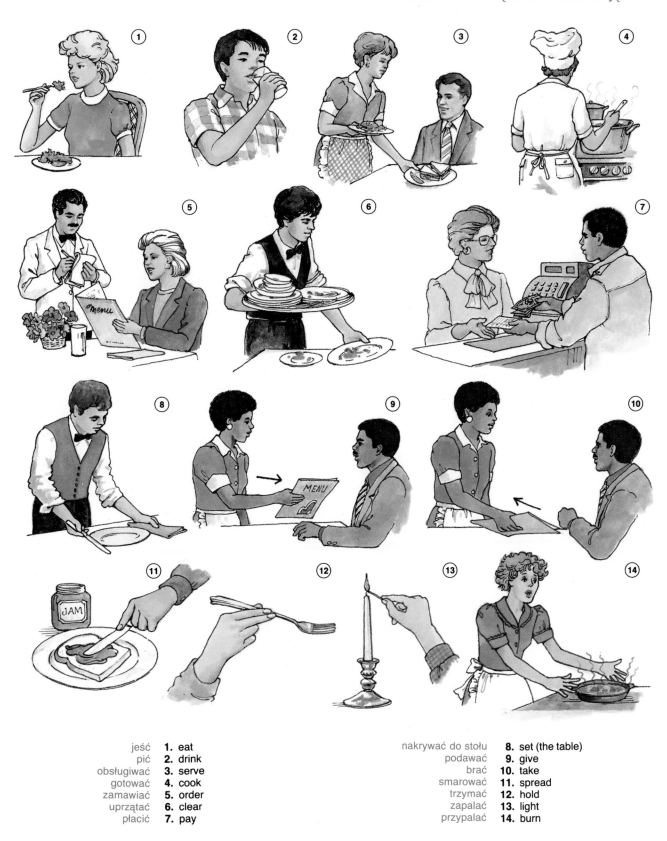

jeść	**1.**	eat
pić	**2.**	drink
obsługiwać	**3.**	serve
gotować	**4.**	cook
zamawiać	**5.**	order
uprzątać	**6.**	clear
płacić	**7.**	pay

nakrywać do stołu	**8.**	set (the table)
podawać	**9.**	give
brać	**10.**	take
smarować	**11.**	spread
trzymać	**12.**	hold
zapalać	**13.**	light
przypalać	**14.**	burn

musztarda	**1.** mustard	pieczony ziemniak	**20.** baked potato
parówka	**2.** hot dog	befsztyk	**21.** steak
zapiekana fasola	**3.** baked beans	ciastka	**22.** cookie
chrupki ziemniaczane	**4.** potato chips	melba	**23.** sundae
naleśniki	**5.** pancakes	meksykański placek	**24.** taco
syrop	**6.** syrup	krokiet	**25.** egg roll
bułka	**7.** bun	kruche ciasto z truskawkami	**26.** strawberry shortcake
ogórek konserwowy	**8.** pickle	sucharek	**27.** biscuit
hamburger	**9.** hamburger	frytki	**28.** french fries
spaghetti	**10.** spaghetti	kurczak smażony	**29.** fried chicken
pulpety	**11.** meatballs	pizza	**30.** pizza
sos do sałaty	**12.** salad dressing	galaretka	**31.** jelly
sałatka mieszana	**13.** tossed salad	jajko (sadzone)	**32.** (sunnyside-up) egg
wołowina duszona	**14.** beef stew	boczek, bekon	**33.** bacon
kotlety schabowe	**15.** pork chops	grzanka	**34.** toast
mieszanka warzywna	**16.** mixed vegetables	kawa	**35.** coffee
puree z ziemniaków	**17.** mashed potatoes	lody w waflu	**36.** ice cream cone
masło	**18.** butter		
kajzerka	**19.** roll		

rękawiczki	**1.** gloves		rajtuzy	**14.** tights
czapka	**2.** cap		łyżwy	**15.** ice skates
koszula flanelowa	**3.** flannel shirt		czapka narciarska	**16.** ski cap
plecak	**4.** backpack		bluza	**17.** jacket
wiatrówka	**5.** windbreaker		kapelusz	**18.** hat
dżinsy	**6.** (blue) jeans		szal	**19.** scarf
sweter z półgolfem	**7.** (crewneck) sweater		płaszcz	**20.** overcoat
skafander	**8.** parka		długie buty	**21.** boots
pionierki, himalaje	**9.** hiking boots		beret	**22.** beret
nauszniki	**10.** earmuffs		sweter (w serek)	**23.** (V-neck) sweater
rękawiczki z jednym palcem	**11.** mittens		kurtka	**24.** coat
kamizelka puchowa	**12.** down vest		śniegowce	**25.** rain boots
sweter (z golfem)	**13.** (turtleneck) sweater			

klapa	**1.** lapel	szorty	**14.** shorts
marynarka	**2.** blazer	długi rękaw	**15.** long sleeve
guzik	**3.** button	pasek	**16.** belt
spodnie	**4.** slacks	sprzączka	**17.** buckle
obcas	**5.** heel	torba na zakupy	**18.** shopping bag
podeszwa	**6.** sole	sandał	**19.** sandal
sznurowadło	**7.** shoelace	kołnierz	**20.** collar
bluza od dresu	**8.** sweatshirt	krótki rękaw	**21.** short sleeve
portfel	**9.** wallet	sukienka	**22.** dress
spodnie od dresu	**10.** sweatpants	torebka	**23.** purse
buty sportowe, tenisówki	**11.** sneakers	parasolka	**24.** umbrella
opaska	**12.** sweatband	(wysokie) obcasy	**25.** (high) heels
koszulka gimnastyczna	**13.** tank top		

blezer	**26.** cardigan	płaszcz przeciwdeszczowy	**38.** raincoat
spodnie (sztruksowe)	**27.** (corduroy) pants	kamizelka	**39.** vest
kask roboczy	**28.** hard hat	garnitur trzyczęściowy	**40.** three-piece suit
podkoszulka	**29.** T-shirt	kieszeń	**41.** pocket
kombinezon, ogrodniczki	**30.** overalls	mokasyn	**42.** loafer
śniadaniówka	**31.** lunch box	czapka	**43.** cap
buty robocze	**32.** (construction) boots	okulary	**44.** glasses
żakiet	**33.** jacket	mundur	**45.** uniform
bluzka	**34.** blouse	koszula	**46.** shirt
torba (na ramię)	**35.** (shoulder) bag	krawat	**47.** tie
spódnica	**36.** skirt	gazeta	**48.** newspaper
teczka, aktówka	**37.** briefcase	but	**49.** shoe

podkoszulka	**1.** undershirt		majteczki (bikini)	**11.** (bikini) panties
szorty	**2.** boxer shorts		majtki	**12.** briefs
slipy	**3.** underpants		stanik	**13.** bra(ssiere)
suspensorium	**4.** athletic supporter		pasek do podwiązek	**14.** garter belt
rajstopy	**5.** pantyhose		pas elastyczny	**15.** girdle
pończochy	**6.** stockings		podkolanówki	**16.** knee socks
ciepła bielizna	**7.** long johns		skarpety	**17.** socks
półhalka	**8.** half slip		pantofle ranne	**18.** slippers
koszulka	**9.** camisole		piżama	**19.** pajamas
halka	**10.** full slip		płaszcz kąpielowy	**20.** bathrobe
			koszula nocna	**21.** nightgown

Biżuteria	**A. Jewelry**	Przybory toaletowe i kosmetyczne	**B. Toiletries and Makeup**
kolczyk	**1.** earrings	maszynka do golenia	**20.** razor
pierścionek	**2.** ring(s)	płyn po goleniu	**21.** after-shave lotion
pierścionek zaręczynowy	**3.** engagement ring	krem do golenia	**22.** shaving cream
obrączka	**4.** wedding ring	żyletki	**23.** razor blades
łańcuszek z wisiorkiem	**5.** chain	pilnik do paznokci	**24.** emery board
naszyjnik	**6.** necklace	lakier do paznokci	**25.** nail polish
(sznur) paciorków	**7.** (strand of) beads	ołówek do brwi	**26.** eyebrow pencil
szpilka	**8.** pin	perfumy	**27.** perfume
bransoleta	**9.** bracelet	tusz do rzęs	**28.** mascara
zegarek	**10.** watch	szminka	**29.** lipstick
pasek do zegarka	**11.** watchband	cień do powiek	**30.** eye shadow
spinki do mankietów	**12.** cuff links	cążki do paznokci	**31.** nail clippers
szpilka do krawata	**13.** tie pin	róż	**32.** blush
spinka do krawata	**14.** tie clip	tusz do oczu	**33.** eyeliner
klips	**15.** clip-on earring		
kolczyk	**16.** pierced earring		
zapięcie	**17.** clasp		
sztyft	**18.** post		
zatrzask	**19.** back		

krótki	**1.** short		płaski, niski	**12.** low
długi	**2.** long		nowy	**13.** new
ciasny	**3.** tight		stary	**14.** old
luźny	**4.** loose		otwarty	**15.** open
brudny	**5.** dirty		zamknięty	**16.** closed
czysty	**6.** clean		w paski	**17.** striped
mały	**7.** small		w kratkę	**18.** checked
duży	**8.** big		w groszki	**19.** polka dot
jasny	**9.** light		gładki	**20.** solid
ciemny	**10.** dark		wzorzysty	**21.** print
wysoki	**11.** high		w szkocką kratę	**22.** plaid

deszczowa	**1.** rainy
pochmurna	**2.** cloudy
śnieżna	**3.** snowy
słoneczna	**4.** sunny
termometr	**5.** thermometer
temperatura	**6.** temperature
gorąco	**7.** hot
ciepło	**8.** warm

chłodno	**9.** cool
zimno	**10.** cold
punkt zamarzania	**11.** freezing
mgliście	**12.** foggy
wietrznie	**13.** windy
sucho	**14.** dry
mokro	**15.** wet
mroźnie	**16.** icy

Czasowniki związane z porami roku

Wiosna	Spring	Lato	Summer	Jesień	Fall	Zima	Winter
malować	**1.** paint	podlewać	**5.** water	napełniać	**9.** fill	odgarniać	**13.** shovel
czyścić	**2.** clean	kosić	**6.** mow	grabić	**10.** rake	posypywać piaskiem	**14.** sand
kopać	**3.** dig	zrywać	**7.** pick	rąbać	**11.** chop	zdrapywać	**15.** scrape
sadzić	**4.** plant	przycinać	**8.** trim	pchać	**12.** push	nosić	**16.** carry

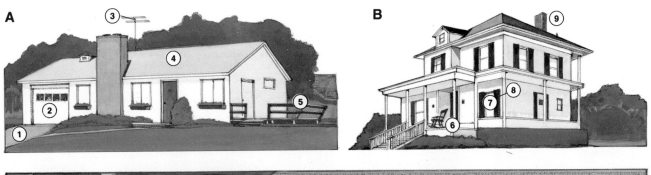

Dom na farmie	**A. Ranch House**
podjazd	**1.** driveway
garaż	**2.** garage
antena telewizyjna	**3.** TV antenna
dach	**4.** roof
taras	**5.** deck
Dom w stylu kolonialnym	**B. Colonial-style House**
ganek	**6.** porch
okno	**7.** window
okiennica	**8.** shutter
komin	**9.** chimney
Podwórko za domem	**C. The Backyard**
rynna pozioma	**10.** gutter
hamak	**11.** hammock
kosiarka do trawy	**12.** lawn mower
rozpryskiwacz	**13.** sprinkler
wąż ogrodowy	**14.** garden hose

trawnik	**15.** grass
konewka	**16.** watering can
patio	**17.** patio
rynna ściekowa	**18.** drainpipe
siatka	**19.** screen
rękawica	**20.** mitt
łopatka	**21.** spatula
grill	**22.** grill
węgiel drzewny w brykietach	**23.** charcoal briquettes
leżanka	**24.** lounge chair
piła mechaniczna	**25.** power saw
rękawice robocze	**26.** work gloves
kielnia	**27.** trowel
składzik na narzędzia	**28.** toolshed
sekator	**29.** hedge clippers
grabie	**30.** rake
łopata	**31.** shovel
taczka	**32.** wheelbarrow

wentylator sufitowy	**1.** ceiling fan	fotel odchylany	**16.** recliner
sufit	**2.** ceiling	pilot	**17.** remote control
ściana	**3.** wall	telewizor	**18.** television
rama	**4.** frame	regał	**19.** wall unit
obraz	**5.** painting	zestaw stereofoniczny	**20.** stereo system
wazon	**6.** vase	głośnik	**21.** speaker
półka nad kominkiem	**7.** mantel	biblioteczka	**22.** bookcase
kominek	**8.** fireplace	zasłony	**23.** drapes
ogień	**9.** fire	poduszka	**24.** cushion
polano	**10.** log	kanapa	**25.** sofa
poręcz	**11.** banister	ława	**26.** coffee table
schody	**12.** staircase	abażur	**27.** lampshade
stopień	**13.** step	lampa	**28.** lamp
biurko	**14.** desk	stolik podręczny	**29.** end table
wykładzina, dywan	**15.** wall-to-wall carpeting		

porcelana, zastawa	**1.** china	obrus	**16.** tablecloth
kredens	**2.** china closet	krzesło	**17.** chair
żyrandol	**3.** chandelier	dzbanek do kawy	**18.** coffeepot
dzbanek	**4.** pitcher	dzbanek do herbaty	**19.** teapot
kieliszek do wina	**5.** wine glass	filiżanka	**20.** cup
kieliszek na wodę	**6.** water glass	spodek	**21.** saucer
stół	**7.** table	sztućce	**22.** silverware
łyżka	**8.** spoon	cukiernica	**23.** sugar bowl
pieprzniczka	**9.** pepper shaker	dzbanuszek na śmietanę	**24.** creamer
solniczka	**10.** salt shaker	salaterka	**25.** salad bowl
talerzyk na chleb z masłem	**11.** bread and butter plate	płomień	**26.** flame
widelec	**12.** fork	świeczka	**27.** candle
talerz	**13.** plate	lichtarz	**28.** candlestick
serwetka	**14.** napkin	pomocnik	**29.** buffet
nóż	**15.** knife		

Kuchnia

zmywarka do naczyń	**1.** dishwasher
suszarka	**2.** dish drainer
wkładka do gotowania na parze	**3.** steamer
otwieracz do konserw	**4.** can opener
patelnia	**5.** frying pan
otwieracz do butelek	**6.** bottle opener
cedzak	**7.** colander
rondel	**8.** saucepan
pokrywka	**9.** lid
płyn do mycia naczyń	**10.** dishwashing liquid
myjka	**11.** scouring pad
mikser	**12.** blender
garnek	**13.** pot
garnek na potrawkę	**14.** casserole dish
pojemnik	**15.** canister
opiekacz do grzanek	**16.** toaster
blacha do pieczenia	**17.** roasting pan

ścierka do naczń	**18.** dish towel
lodówka	**19.** refrigerator
zamrażarka	**20.** freezer
pojemnik na lód	**21.** ice tray
szafka	**22.** cabinet
kuchnia mikrofalowa	**23.** microwave oven
donica do mieszania	**24.** mixing bowl
wałek	**25.** rolling pin
deska	**26.** cutting board
blat	**27.** counter
czajnik	**28.** teakettle
palnik	**29.** burner
kuchenka	**30.** stove
dzbanek do robienia kawy	**31.** coffeemaker
piecyk	**32.** oven
opiekacz	**33.** broiler
ochraniacz, trzymacz do garnków	**34.** pot holder

Czasowniki związane z kuchnią

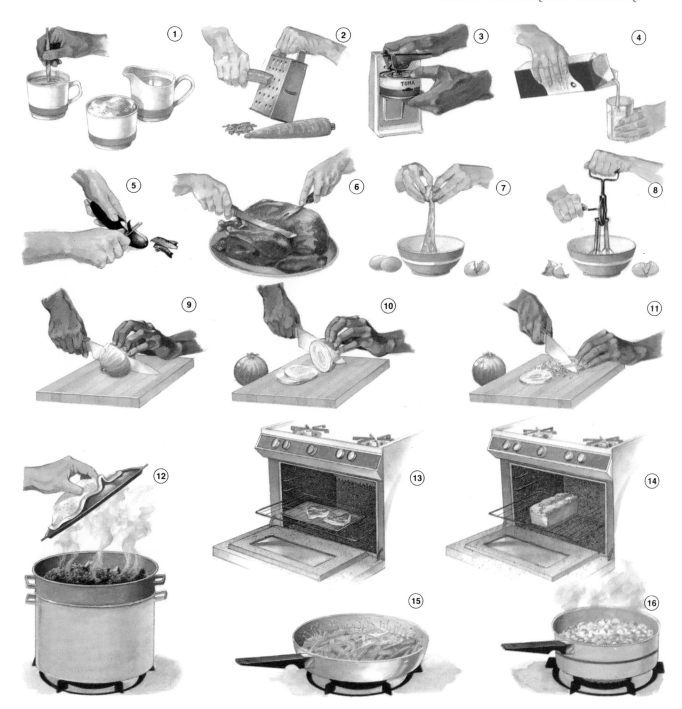

mieszać	**1.** stir		kroić, ciąć	**9.** cut
trzeć	**2.** grate		ciąć w plasterki	**10.** slice
otwierać	**3.** open		szatkować	**11.** chop
nalewać	**4.** pour		gotować na parze	**12.** steam
obierać	**5.** peel		opiekać	**13.** broil
kroić	**6.** carve		piec	**14.** bake
rozbijać	**7.** break		smażyć	**15.** fry
ubijać	**8.** beat		gotować	**16.** boil

wieszak, haczyk	**1.** hook		materac	**17.** mattress
ramiączko, wieszak	**2.** hanger		sprężyny	**18.** box spring
szafa w ścianie	**3.** closet		prześcieradło	**19.** (flat) sheet
szkatułka, kaseta na biżuterię	**4.** jewelry box		koc	**20.** blanket
lustro	**5.** mirror		łóżko	**21.** bed
grzebień	**6.** comb		przykrycie na nogi	**22.** comforter
szczotka do włosów	**7.** hairbrush		narzuta	**23.** bedspread
budzik	**8.** alarm clock		szczyt krótki	**24.** footboard
komoda (toaletka)	**9.** bureau		kontakt	**25.** light switch
zasłona	**10.** curtain		telefon	**26.** phone
klimatyzator	**11.** air conditioner		sznur	**a.** cord
żaluzje	**12.** blinds		wtyczka	**b.** jack
chusteczki papierowe	**13.** tissues		stolik nocny	**27.** night table
szczyt długi	**14.** headboard		dywan	**28.** rug
powłoczka na poduszkę	**15.** pillowcase		podłoga	**29.** floor
poduszka	**16.** pillow		komoda	**30.** chest of drawers

roleta	**1.** shade	butelka	**17.** bottle
mobil	**2.** mobile	smoczek	**18.** nipple
miś	**3.** teddy bear	śpioszki	**19.** stretchie
łóżeczko dziecięce	**4.** crib	śliniak	**20.** bib
szczebel	**5.** bumper	grzechotka	**21.** rattle
oliwka	**6.** baby lotion	smoczek	**22.** pacifier
zasypka	**7.** baby powder	chodzik	**23.** walker
chusteczki	**8.** baby wipes	huśtawka	**24.** swing
stolik do przebierania	**9.** changing table	dom dla lalek	**25.** doll house
waciki	**10.** cotton swab	kołyska	**26.** cradle
agrafka	**11.** safety pin	pluszowe zwierzątko	**27.** stuffed animal
pieluszki jednorazowe	**12.** disposable diaper	lalka	**28.** doll
pieluszki płócienne	**13.** cloth diaper	pudło z zabawkami	**29.** toy chest
wózek spacerowy	**14.** stroller	kojec	**30.** playpen
wykrywacz dymu	**15.** smoke detector	układanka	**31.** puzzle
bujak	**16.** rocking chair	klocek	**32.** block
		nocnik	**33.** potty

karnisz, drążek na zasłonę	**1.** curtain rod	kurek ciepłej wody	**17.** hot water faucet
kółka	**2.** curtain rings	kurek zimnej wody	**18.** cold water faucet
czepek kąpielowy	**3.** shower cap	umywalka	**19.** sink
sitko prysznica	**4.** shower head	szczotka do paznokci	**20.** nailbrush
zasłona	**5.** shower curtain	szczotka do zębów	**21.** toothbrush
mydelniczka	**6.** soap dish	myjka	**22.** washcloth
gąbka	**7.** sponge	ręcznik	**23.** hand towel
szampon	**8.** shampoo	ręcznik kąpielowy	**24.** bath towel
otwór przelewowy	**9.** drain	wieszak na ręczniki	**25.** towel rack
korek	**10.** stopper	suszarka do włosów	**26.** hair dryer
wanna	**11.** bathtub	glazura	**27.** tile
mata	**12.** bath mat	kosz z pokrywką	**28.** hamper
kosz na śmieci	**13.** wastepaper basket	muszla klozetowa	**29.** toilet
apteczka	**14.** medicine chest	papier toaletowy	**30.** toilet paper
mydło	**15.** soap	szczotka klozetowa	**31.** toilet brush
pasta do zębów	**16.** toothpaste	waga	**32.** scale

drabina	**1.** stepladder	rura	**18.** pipe
skurzawka	**2.** feather duster	sznur do bielizny	**19.** clothesline
latarka	**3.** flashlight	spinacze do bielizny	**20.** clothespins
ścierki, szmaty	**4.** rags	krochmal w spray'u	**21.** spray starch
bezpiecznik	**5.** circuit breaker	żarówka	**22.** lightbulb
myjka do podłogi (z gąbką)	**6.** (sponge) mop	ręcznik papierowy	**23.** paper towels
miotła	**7.** broom	suszarka	**24.** dryer
śmietniczka	**8.** dustpan	proszek do prania	**25.** laundry detergent
proszek do szorowania	**9.** cleanser	bielinka	**26.** bleach
środek do mycia okien	**10.** window cleaner	płyn do płukania	**27.** fabric softener
wkład do myjki	**11.** (mop) refill	bielizna do prania	**28.** laundry
żelazko	**12.** iron	kosz na bieliznę	**29.** laundry basket
deska do prasowania	**13.** ironing board	pralka	**30.** washing machine
przetykacz do zlewów	**14.** plunger	pojemnik na śmieci	**31.** garbage can
wiadro	**15.** bucket	pułapka na myszy	**32.** mousetrap
odkurzacz	**16.** vacuum cleaner		
ssawki do odkurzacza	**17.** attachments		

calówka	**1.** carpenter's rule	młotek	**13.** hammer
ścisk stolarski	**2.** C-clamp	szpachla	**14.** scraper
wycinarka	**3.** jigsaw	tablica narzędziowa	**15.** pegboard
drewno	**4.** wood	haczyk	**16.** hook
przedłużacz	**5.** extension cord	toporek	**17.** hatchet
gniazdko	**6.** outlet	piłka do metalu	**18.** hacksaw
wtyczka z uziemieniem	**7.** grounding plug	kombinerki	**19.** pliers
piła	**8.** saw	piła tarczowa	**20.** circular saw
korba	**9.** brace	miarka taśmowa	**21.** tape measure
klucz nastawny	**10.** wrench	stół warsztatowy	**22.** workbench
młotek gumowy	**11.** mallet	pudło na narzędzia	**23.** toolbox
klucz nastawny pojedyńczy	**12.** monkey wrench		

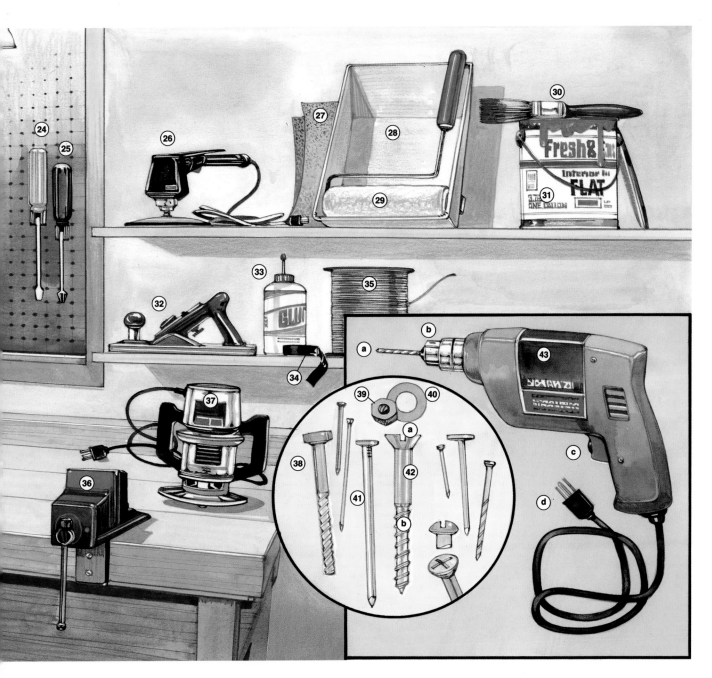

śrubokręt	**24.** screwdriver		frez ręczny	**37.** router
śrubokręt krzyżakowy	**25.** Phillips screwdriver		śruba	**38.** bolt
szlifierka elektryczna	**26.** power sander		nakrętka	**39.** nut
papier ścierny	**27.** sandpaper		podkładka	**40.** washer
kuweta	**28.** pan		gwóźdź	**41.** nail
wałek	**29.** roller		wkręt	**42.** screw
pędzel do malowania	**30.** paintbrush		łeb	**a.** head
farba	**31.** paint		gwint	**b.** thread
strug	**32.** wood plane		wiertarka elektryczna	**43.** electric drill
klej	**33.** glue		wiertło	**a.** bit
taśma izolacyjna	**34.** electrical tape		uchwyt	**b.** shank
drut	**35.** wire		włącznik	**c.** switch
imadło	**36.** vise		wtyczka	**d.** plug

Czasowniki związane z pracami domowymi i naprawą

składać	**1.** fold	wycierać (do sucha)	**9.** dry
szorować	**2.** scrub	reperować	**10.** repair
polerować	**3.** polish	prasować	**11.** iron
dokręcać	**4.** tighten	oliwić	**12.** oil
wycierać na mokro	**5.** wipe	zmieniać (pościel)	**13.** change (the sheets)
wieszać	**6.** hang	odkurzać	**14.** vacuum
zamiatać	**7.** sweep	ścierać kurze	**15.** dust
ścielić	**8.** make (the bed)	prać	**16.** wash

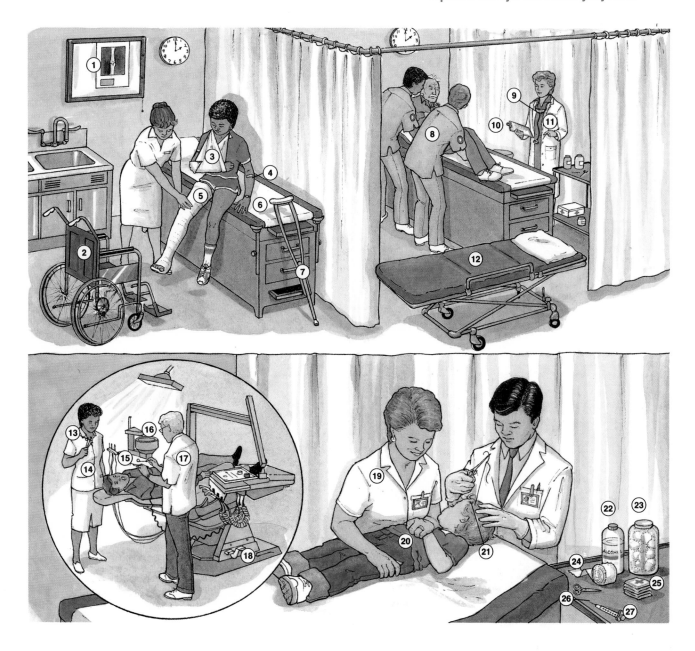

prześwietlenie	**1.** X-ray	bor	**15.** drill
fotel na kółkach	**2.** wheelchair	spluwaczka	**16.** basin
temblak	**3.** sling	dentysta	**17.** dentist
plaster	**4.** Band-Aid	pedał	**18.** pedal
gips	**5.** cast	pielęgniarka	**19.** nurse
stół do badania	**6.** examining table	pacjent	**20.** patient
kule	**7.** crutch	szwy	**21.** stitches
sanitariusz	**8.** attendant	spirytus	**22.** alcohol
stetoskop	**9.** stethoscope	waciki	**23.** cotton balls
karta choroby	**10.** chart	bandaż (gazowy)	**24.** (gauze) bandage
lekarz	**11.** doctor	gaziki	**25.** gauze pads
nosze	**12.** stretcher	igła	**26.** needle
instrumenty	**13.** instruments	strzykawka	**27.** syringe
pomoc stomatologiczna	**14.** oral hygienist		

wysypka	**1.** rash	przeziębienie	**11.** cold
gorączka	**2.** fever	ból gardła	**12.** sore throat
ukąszenie owada	**3.** insect bite	szpatułka	**a.** tongue depressor
dreszcze	**4.** chills	zwichnięcie	**13.** sprain
podbite oko	**5.** black eye	bandaż elastyczny	**a.** stretch bandage
ból głowy	**6.** headache	infekcja	**14.** infection
ból brzucha	**7.** stomachache	złamana kość	**15.** broken bone
ból pleców	**8.** backache	skaleczenie	**16.** cut
ból zęba	**9.** toothache	stłuczenie	**17.** bruise
wysokie ciśnienie	**10.** high blood pressure	oparzenie	**18.** burn

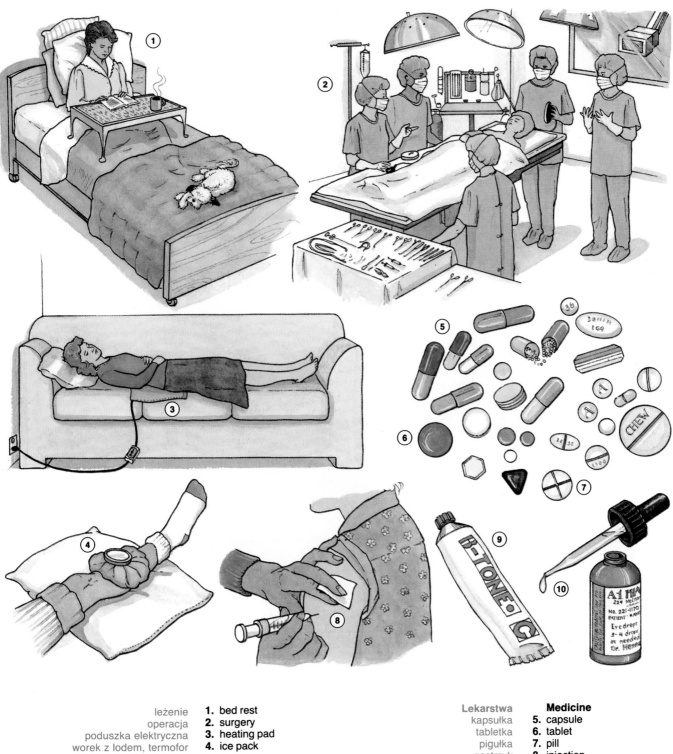

leżenie	**1.** bed rest		
operacja	**2.** surgery		
poduszka elektryczna	**3.** heating pad		
worek z lodem, termofor	**4.** ice pack		

Lekarstwa	**Medicine**
kapsułka	**5.** capsule
tabletka	**6.** tablet
pigułka	**7.** pill
zastrzyk	**8.** injection
maść	**9.** ointment
krople do oczu	**10.** eye drops

drabina	**1.** ladder		hydrant	**9.** fire hydrant
wóz pożarniczy	**2.** fire engine		strażak	**10.** fire fighter
motopompa	**3.** fire truck		gaśnica	**11.** fire extinguisher
schody ewakuacyjne	**4.** fire escape		hełm	**12.** helmet
ogień	**5.** fire		płaszcz	**13.** coat
karetka	**6.** ambulance		topór	**14.** ax
sanitariusz	**7.** paramedic		dym	**15.** smoke
wąż	**8.** hose		woda	**16.** water
			dysza	**17.** nozzle

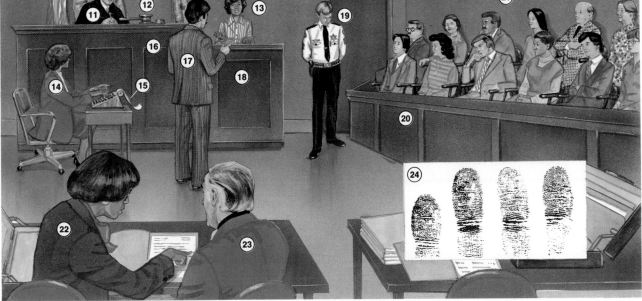

Posterunek policji	**A. Police Station**
areszt	**1.** jail
agent policji	**2.** detective
podejrzany	**3.** suspect
kajdanki	**4.** handcuffs
odznaka	**5.** badge
policjant	**6.** police officer
rewolwer	**7.** gun
kabura	**8.** holster
pałka	**9.** nightstick
Sąd	**B. Court**
sędzia	**10.** judge
toga	**11.** robes

młotek	**12.** gavel
świadek	**13.** witness
protokolant	**14.** court reporter
protokół	**15.** transcript
trybunał	**16.** bench
prokurator	**17.** prosecuting attorney
miejsce dla świadka	**18.** witness stand
strażnik sądowy	**19.** court officer
ława przysięgłych	**20.** jury box
przysięgli	**21.** jury
adwokat, obrońca	**22.** defense attorney
podsądny	**23.** defendant
odciski palców	**24.** fingerprints

biurowiec	**1.** office building	poczta	**9.** post office
hall	**2.** lobby	policjant drogowy	**10.** traffic cop
róg	**3.** corner	skrzyżowanie	**11.** intersection
przejście dla pieszych	**4.** crosswalk	pieszy	**12.** pedestrian
dom towarowy	**5.** department store	przystanek autobusowy	**13.** bus stop
piekarnia	**6.** bakery	ławka	**14.** bench
automat telefoniczny	**7.** public telephone	kosz na śmieci	**15.** trash basket
znak drogowy	**8.** street sign	stacja metra	**16.** subway station

winda	**17.** elevator	chodnik	**25.** sidewalk
księgarnia	**18.** bookstore	krawężnik	**26.** curb
parking	**19.** parking garage	wózek dziecięcy	**27.** baby carriage
parkometr	**20.** parking meter	sklep warzywny	**28.** fruit and vegetable market
sygnalizacja świetlna	**21.** traffic light	latarnia uliczna	**29.** streetlight
apteka	**22.** drugstore	kiosk z gazetami	**30.** newsstand
dom mieszkalny	**23.** apartment house	ulica	**31.** street
numer budynku	**24.** building number	właz	**32.** manhole

Doręczanie poczty	**A. Delivering Mail**	urzędnik pocztowy	14. postal worker
skrzynka na listy	1. mailbox	okienko	15. window
przesyłki	2. mail		
doręczyciel	3. letter carrier	**Rodzaje przesyłek**	**C. Types of Mail**
torba na listy	4. mailbag	koperta (lotnicza)	16. (airmail) envelope
furgon pocztowy	5. mail truck	karta pocztowa	17. postcard
skrzynka pocztowa	6. U.S. mailbox	przekaz pieniężny	18. money order
list	7. letter	paczka	19. package
adres zwrotny	8. return address	sznurek	20. string
stempel	9. postmark	nalepka	21. label
znaczek pocztowy	10. stamp	taśma	22. tape
adres	11. address	przesyłka Poczty Ekspresowej	23. Express Mail (package)
kod pocztowy	12. zip code		

Urząd pocztowy   **B. The Post Office**

wrzut listów   13. mail slot

bibliotekarka	**1.** library clerk	dział czasopism	**15.** periodicals section
wypożyczalnia	**2.** checkout desk	magazyn ilustrowany	**16.** magazine
karta biblioteczna	**3.** library card	półka, stojak	**17.** rack
katalog	**4.** card catalog	fotokopiarka	**18.** photocopy machine
szuflada	**5.** drawer	globus	**19.** globe
karta katalogowa	**6.** call card	atlas	**20.** atlas
sygnatura	**7.** call number	księgozbiór podręczny	**21.** reference section
autor	**8.** author	informacja	**22.** information desk
tytuł	**9.** title	bibliotekarka (działu podręcznego)	**23.** (reference) librarian
dział	**10.** subject	słownik	**24.** dictionary
regał	**11.** row	encyklopedia	**25.** encyclopedia
rewers	**12.** call slip	półka	**26.** shelf
mikrofilm	**13.** microfilm		
czytnik mikrofilmów	**14.** microfilm reader		

Siły zbrojne

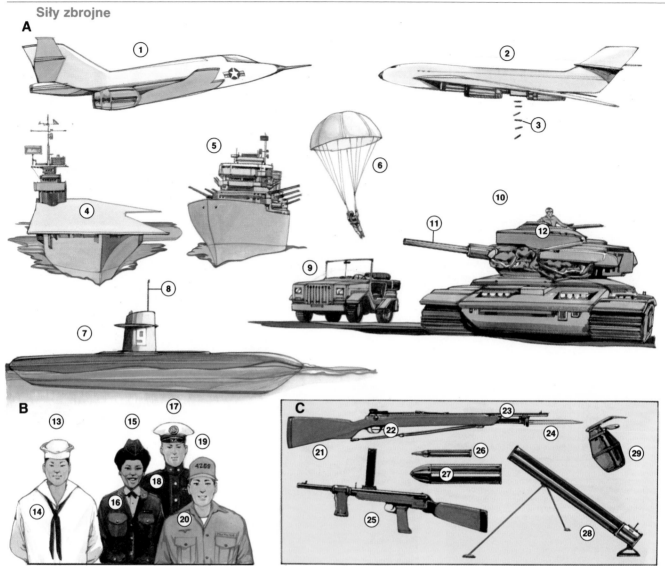

Pojazdy i sprzęt	**A. Vehicles and Equipment**
samolot myśliwski	**1.** fighter plane
bombowiec	**2.** bomber
bomba	**3.** bomb
lotniskowiec	**4.** aircraft carrier
pancernik	**5.** battleship
spadochron	**6.** parachute
łódź podwodna	**7.** submarine
peryskop	**8.** periscope
samochód terenowy	**9.** jeep
czołg	**10.** tank
działo	**11.** cannon
wieżyczka	**12.** gun turret

Personel	**B. Personnel**
marynarka	**13.** Navy
marynarz	**14.** sailor
siły lądowe	**15.** Army

żołnierz	**16.** soldier
piechota morska	**17.** Marines
żołnierz piechoty morskiej	**18.** marine
lotnictwo	**19.** Air Force
lotnik	**20.** airman

Broń i amunicja	**C. Weapons and Ammunition**
karabin	**21.** rifle
spust	**22.** trigger
lufa	**23.** barrel
bagnet	**24.** bayonet
pistolet maszynowy	**25.** machine gun
kula	**26.** bullet
nabój	**27.** shell
moździerz	**28.** mortar
granat ręczny	**29.** hand grenade

zamiatarka uliczna	**1.** street cleaner	konwojent	**10.** delivery person
pojazd holowniczy	**2.** tow truck	samochód do przeprowadzek	**11.** moving van
cysterna z paliwem	**3.** fuel truck	pracownik transportowy	**12.** mover
pick-up	**4.** pickup truck	gruszka do betonu	**13.** cement truck
pług śnieżny	**5.** snow plow	wywrotka	**14.** dump truck
śmieciarka	**6.** garbage truck	ciągnik siodłowy	**15.** tractor trailer
pracownik oczyszczania miasta	**7.** sanitation worker	kierowca ciężarówki	**16.** truck driver
ruchomy punkt żywienia	**8.** lunch truck	lora samochodowa	**17.** transporter
furgon	**9.** panel truck	platforma	**18.** flatbed

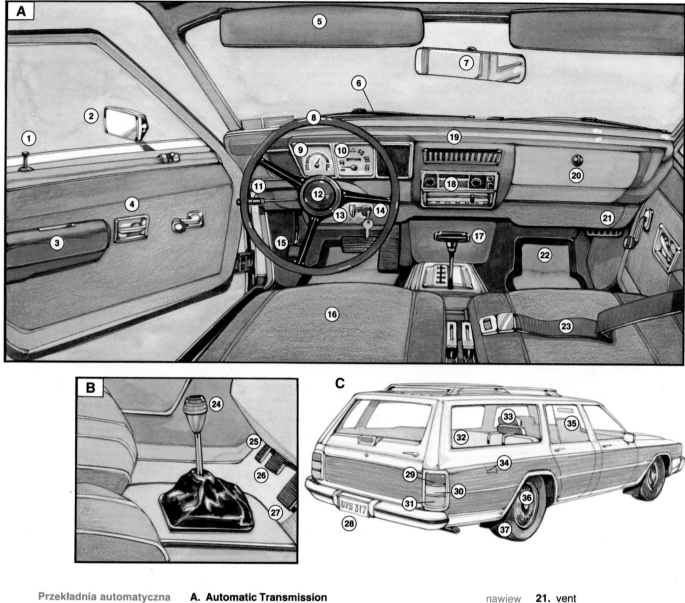

Przekładnia automatyczna	A. Automatic Transmission		nawiew	21. vent
blokada drzwi	1. door lock		dywanik	22. mat
lusterko boczne	2. side mirror		pas bezpieczeństwa	23. seat belt
podłokietnik	3. armrest			
klamka	4. door handle		**Przekładnia ręczna**	**B. Manual Transmission**
daszek	5. visor		dźwignia zmiany biegów	24. stick shift
wycieraczka	6. windshield wiper		sprzęgło	25. clutch
lusterko wsteczne	7. rearview mirror		hamulec	26. brake
kierownica	8. steering wheel		pedał gazu	27. accelerator
wskaźnik poziomu paliwa	9. gas gauge			
szybkościomierz	10. speedometer		**Kombi**	**C. Station Wagon**
dźwignia migaczy	11. turn signal lever		numer rejestracyjny	28. license plate
klakson	12. horn		światło stopu	29. brake light
kolumna kierownicza	13. column		światło cofania	30. backup light
stacyjka	14. ignition		światło pozycyjne tylne	31. taillight
hamulec ręczny	15. emergency brake		siedzenie tylne	32. backseat
fotel kubełkowy	16. bucket seat		siedzenie dla dziecka	33. child's seat
dźwignia zmiany biegów	17. gearshift		zbiornik paliwa	34. gas tank
radio	18. radio		zagłówek	35. headrest
deska rozdzielcza	19. dashboard		dekiel	36. hubcap
schowek	20. glove compartment		opona	37. tire

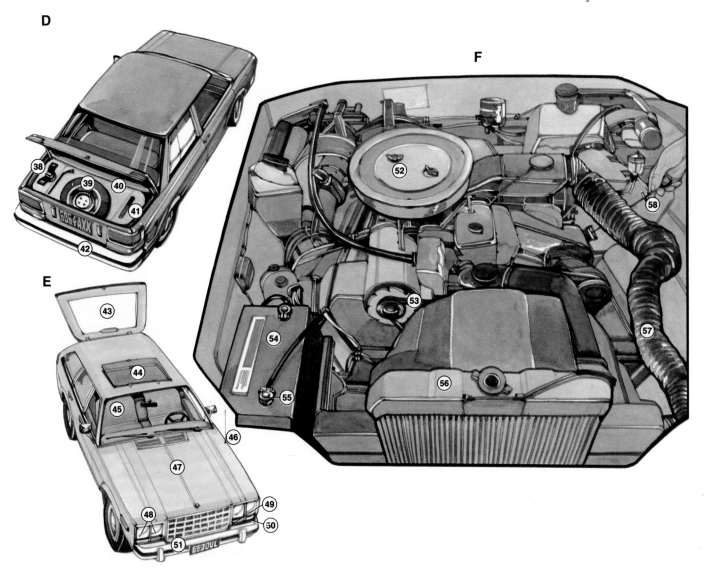

D

E

F

Sedan dwudrzwiowy	**D. (Two-door) Sedan**
podnośnik	**38.** jack
koło zapasowe	**39.** spare tire
bagażnik	**40.** trunk
flara ostrzegawcza	**41.** flare
tylny zderzak	**42.** rear bumper
Czterodrzwiowy z tylną klapą	**E. Four-door Hatchback**
tylna klapa	**43.** hatchback
otwierany dach	**44.** sunroof
szyba przednia	**45.** windshield
antena	**46.** antenna
pokrywa silnika	**47.** hood
reflektory	**48.** headlights

światła pozycyjne	**49.** parking lights
migacze	**50.** turn signal (lights)
zderzak przedni	**51.** front bumper
Silnik	**F. Engine**
filtr powietrza	**52.** air filter
pasek klinowy	**53.** fan belt
akumulator	**54.** battery
końcówka, klema	**55.** terminal
chłodnica	**56.** radiator
wąż	**57.** hose
bagnet	**58.** dipstick

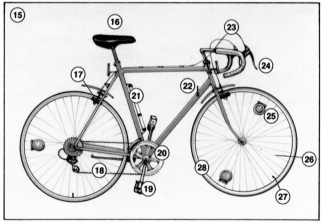

kółka do nauki	**1.** training wheels		łańcuch	**18.** chain
kierownica (kolarska)	**2.** (racing) handlebars		pedał	**19.** pedal
rama damki	**3.** girl's frame		tryb główny	**20.** sprocket
koło	**4.** wheel		pompka	**21.** pump
trąbka, sygnał	**5.** horn		dźwignia przerzutki	**22.** gear changer
trójkołowiec	**6.** tricycle		linka	**23.** cable
kask	**7.** helmet		hamulec ręczny	**24.** hand brake
rower terenowy	**8.** dirt bike		światło odblaskowe	**25.** reflector
nóżka	**9.** kickstand		szprycha	**26.** spoke
błotnik	**10.** fender		wentyl	**27.** valve
rama męska	**11.** boy's frame		opona	**28.** tire
kierownica turystyczna	**12.** touring handlebars		skuter	**29.** motor scooter
kłódka	**13.** lock		motocykl	**30.** motorcycle
stojak na rowery	**14.** bike stand		teleskopy, amortyzatory	**31.** shock absorbers
rower	**15.** bicycle		silnik	**32.** engine
siodełko	**16.** seat		rura wydechowa	**33.** exhaust pipe
hamulec	**17.** brake			

autostrada międzystanowa	**1.** interstate highway	samochód osobowy	**15.** passenger car	
zjazd	**2.** exit ramp	samochód kempingowy	**16.** camper	
wiadukt	**3.** overpass	samochód sportowy	**17.** sports car	
koniczynka	**4.** cloverleaf	bariera	**18.** center divider	
pas lewy	**5.** left lane	motocykl	**19.** motorcycle	
pas środkowy	**6.** center lane	autobus	**20.** bus	
prawy pas	**7.** right lane	wjazd	**21.** entrance ramp	
znak ograniczenia szybkości	**8.** speed limit sign	pobocze	**22.** shoulder	
autostopowicz	**9.** hitchhiker	znak drogowy	**23.** road sign	
przyczepa kampingowa	**10.** trailer	znak zjazdu	**24.** exit sign	
stacja obsługi	**11.** service area	ciężarówka	**25.** truck	
pracownik stacji	**12.** attendant	furgonetka	**26.** van	
sprężarka	**13.** air pump	rogatka, myto	**27.** tollbooth	
dystrybutor	**14.** gas pump			

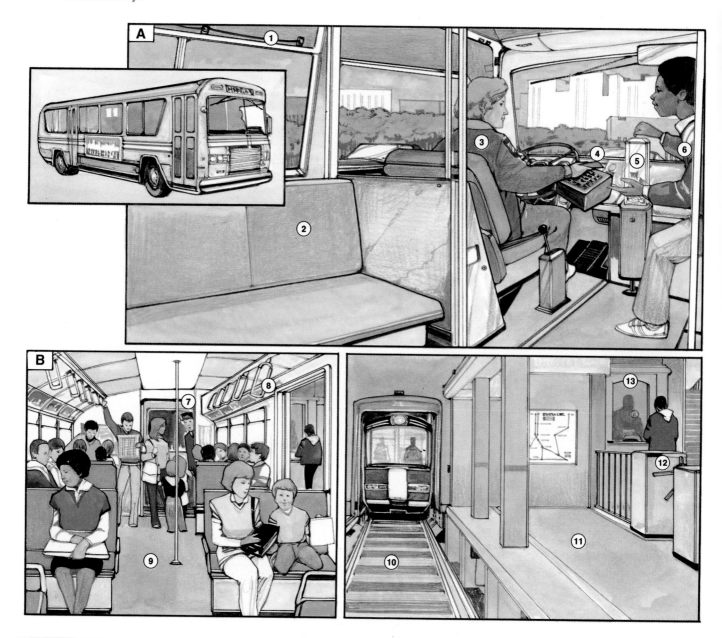

Autobus	A. Bus
sznur	1. cord
miejsce do siedzenia	2. seat
kierowca autobusu	3. bus driver
bilet na przesiadkę	4. transfer
pojemnik na opłatę	5. fare box
pasażer	6. rider

Metro	B. Subway
konduktor	7. conductor
uchwyt	8. strap
wagon	9. car
tory	10. track
peron	11. platform
kołowrotek u wejścia	12. turnstile
okienko z żetonami	13. token booth

Pociąg	C. **Train**
kolejka dojazdowa	**14.** commuter train
maszynista	**15.** engineer
bilet	**16.** ticket
dojeżdżający	**17.** commuter
stacja	**18.** station
kasa biletowa	**19.** ticket window
rozkład jazdu	**20.** timetable

Taksówka	D. **Taxi**
opłata za przejazd	**21.** fare
napiwek	**22.** tip
taksometr	**23.** meter

rachunek	**24.** receipt
pasażer	**25.** passenger
taksówkarz	**26.** cab driver
taksówka	**27.** taxicab
postój taksówek	**28.** taxi stand

Inne środki komunikacji	E. **Other Forms of Transportation**
kolej na jednej szynie	**29.** monorail
tramwaj	**30.** streetcar
kolejka linowa	**31.** aerial tramway
tramwaj linowy	**32.** cable car
powóz konny	**33.** horse-drawn carriage

Odprawa na lotnisku	Airport Check-In	Wejście na pokład	Boarding
torba na ubrania	**1.** garment bag	kabina pilota	**13.** cockpit
bagaż podręczny	**2.** carry-on bag	instrumenty	**14.** instruments
podróżny	**3.** traveler	pilot	**15.** pilot
bilet	**4.** ticket	drugi pilot	**16.** copilot
bagażowy	**5.** porter	mechanik pokładowy	**17.** flight engineer
wózek	**6.** dolly	karta wejścia na pokład	**18.** boarding pass
walizka	**7.** suitcase	kabina	**19.** cabin
bagaż	**8.** baggage	steward	**20.** flight attendant
		pojemnik na bagaż	**21.** luggage compartment
Ochrona	**Security**	stolik opuszczany	**22.** tray table
strażnik	**9.** security guard	przejście	**23.** aisle
wykrywacz metali	**10.** metal detector		
czujnik rentgenowski	**11.** X-ray screener		
taśma	**12.** conveyor belt		

A

B

Rodzaje statków powietrznych	**A. Aircraft Types**	Start	**B. Takeoff**
balon na ciepłe powietrze	**1.** hot air balloon	silnik odrzutowy	**11.** jet engine
helikopter	**2.** helicopter	luk bagażowy	**12.** cargo area
śmigło	**a.** rotor	drzwi ładowni	**13.** cargo door
prywatny odrzutowiec	**3.** private jet	kadłub	**14.** fuselage
szybowiec	**4.** glider	podwozie	**15.** landing gear
sterowiec	**5.** blimp	budynek dworca lotniczego	**16.** terminal building
lotnia	**6.** hang glider	hangar	**17.** hangar
samolot śmigłowy	**7.** propeller plane	odrzutowiec	**18.** (jet) plane
przód	**8.** nose	pas startowy	**19.** runway
skrzydło	**9.** wing	wieża kontrolna	**20.** control tower
ogon	**10.** tail		

łódź rybacka	**1.** fishing boat		boja	**16.** buoy
rybak	**2.** fisherman		prom	**17.** ferry
pirs	**3.** pier		komin	**18.** smokestack
wózek widłowy	**4.** forklift		łódź ratunkowa	**19.** lifeboat
dziób	**5.** bow		trap	**20.** gangway
dźwig	**6.** crane		iluminator, bulaj	**21.** porthole
kontener	**7.** container		pokład	**22.** deck
ładownia	**8.** hold		winda kotwiczna	**23.** windlass
statek (kontenerowy)	**9.** (container)ship		kotwica	**24.** anchor
ładunek	**10.** cargo		cuma	**25.** line
rufa	**11.** stern		pachołek	**26.** bollard
barka	**12.** barge		pasażerski liniowiec oceaniczny	**27.** ocean liner
holownik	**13.** tugboat		dok	**28.** dock
latarnia morska	**14.** lighthouse		dworzec	**29.** terminal
zbiornikowiec	**15.** tanker			

kamizelka	**1.** life jacket	windsurfer	**14.** windsurfer
kanadyjka	**2.** canoe	deska	**15.** sailboard
wiosło	**3.** paddle	jacht motorowy	**16.** cabin cruiser
żaglówka	**4.** sailboat	kajak	**17.** kayak
ster	**5.** rudder	bączek	**18.** dinghy
miecz	**6.** centerboard	miejsce do cumowania	**19.** mooring
bom	**7.** boom	tratwa nadmuchiwana	**20.** inflatable raft
maszt	**8.** mast	dulka	**21.** oarlock
żagiel	**9.** sail	wiosło	**22.** oar
narciarz wodny	**10.** water-skier	łódź wiosłowa	**23.** rowboat
lina holownicza	**11.** towrope		
silnik doczepny	**12.** outboard motor		
motorówka	**13.** motorboat		

Kwiaty	**Flowers**	poinsecja	**15.** poinsettia
tulipan	**1.** tulip	fiołek	**16.** violet
łodyga	**a.** stem	jaskier	**17.** buttercup
bratek	**2.** pansy	róża	**18.** rose
lilia	**3.** lily	pączek	**a.** bud
chryzantema	**4.** (chrysanthe)mum	płatek	**b.** petal
rumianek	**5.** daisy	kolec, cierń	**c.** thorn
aksamitka	**6.** marigold	słonecznik	**19.** sunflower
petunia	**7.** petunia		
żonkil, żółty narcyz	**8.** daffodil	**Trawy i zboża**	**Grasses and Grains**
cebulka	**a.** bulb	trzcina cukrowa	**20.** sugarcane
krokus	**9.** crocus	ryż	**21.** rice
hiacynt	**10.** hyacinth	pszenica	**22.** wheat
irys	**11.** iris	owies	**23.** oats
orchidea	**12.** orchid	kukurydza	**24.** corn
cynia	**13.** zinnia		
gardenia	**14.** gardenia		

Drzewa	Trees
sekwoja	**25.** redwood
palma	**26.** palm
eukaliptus	**27.** eucalyptus
dereń	**28.** dogwood
magnolia	**29.** magnolia
topola	**30.** poplar
wierzba	**31.** willow
brzoza	**32.** birch
dąb	**33.** oak
gałązka	**a.** twig
żołądź	**b.** acorn
sosna	**34.** pine
igła	**a.** needle
szyszka	**b.** cone
drzewo	**35.** tree
konar	**a.** branch
pień	**b.** trunk
kora	**c.** bark
korzeń	**d.** root

wiąz	**36.** elm
liść	**a.** leaf
ostrokrzew	**37.** holly
klon	**38.** maple
Inne rośliny	**Other Plants**
rośliny domowe	**39.** house plants
kaktus	**40.** cactus
krzewy	**41.** bushes
winorośl	**42.** vine
Rośliny trujące	**Poisonous Plants**
dąb jadowity	**43.** poison oak
sumak jadowity	**44.** poison sumac
bluszcz jadowity	**45.** poison ivy

Zwierzęta proste

ślimak	**1.** snail		krewetka	**8.** shrimp
muszla	**a.** shell		krab	**9.** crab
rożek	**b.** antenna		przegrzebek	**10.** scallop
ostryga	**2.** oyster		dżdżownica	**11.** worm
omułek	**3.** mussel		meduza	**12.** jellyfish
ślimak nagi	**4.** slug		czułek	**a.** tentacle
kałamarnica	**5.** squid		homar	**13.** lobster
ośmiornica	**6.** octopus		szczypce	**a.** claw
rozgwiazda	**7.** starfish			

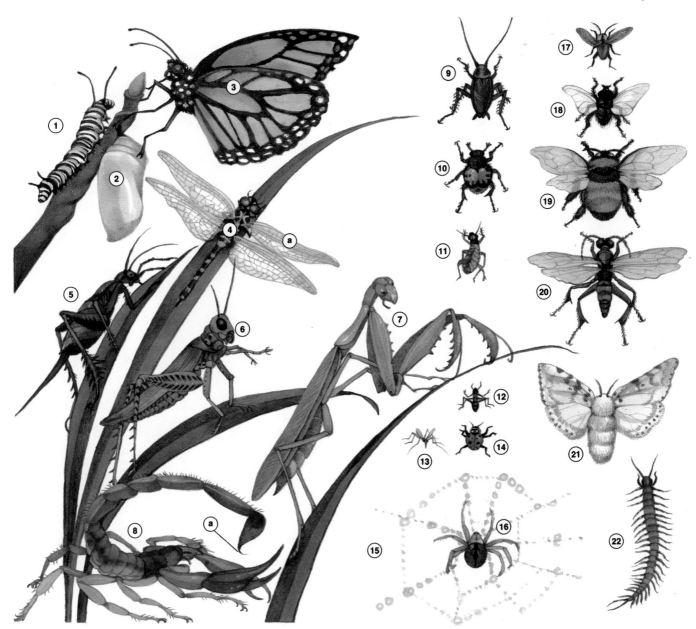

gąsienica	**1.** caterpillar
kokon	**2.** cocoon
motyl	**3.** butterfly
ważka	**4.** dragonfly
skrzydło	**a.** wing
cykada	**5.** cricket
pasikonik	**6.** grasshopper
modliszka	**7.** mantis
skorpion	**8.** scorpion
żądło	**a.** sting
karaczan	**9.** cockroach
chrząszcz, żuk	**10.** beetle
termit	**11.** termite

mrówka	**12.** ant
komar	**13.** mosquito
biedronka	**14.** ladybug
pajęczyna	**15.** web
pająk	**16.** spider
robaczek świętojański	**17.** firefly
mucha	**18.** fly
pszczoła	**19.** bee
osa	**20.** wasp
mól	**21.** moth
stonoga	**22.** centipede

gołąb	**1.** pigeon		papuga	**16.** parrot
skrzydło	**a.** wing		dzięcioł	**17.** woodpecker
koliber	**2.** hummingbird		paw	**18.** peacock
kruk	**3.** crow		bażant	**19.** pheasant
dziób	**a.** beak		indyk	**20.** turkey
mewa	**4.** sea gull		kogut	**21.** rooster
orzeł	**5.** eagle		pisklę	**22.** chick
sowa	**6.** owl		kura	**23.** chicken
jastrząb	**7.** hawk		pelikan	**24.** pelican
pióro	**a.** feather		dziób	**a.** bill
sójka amerykańska	**8.** blue jay		kaczka	**25.** duck
rudzik, drozd wędrowny	**9.** robin		gęś	**26.** goose
wróbel	**10.** sparrow		pingwin	**27.** penguin
kardynał	**11.** cardinal		łabędź	**28.** swan
struś	**12.** ostrich		flaming	**29.** flamingo
jajo	**13.** egg		bocian	**30.** stork
kanarek	**14.** canary		gniazdo	**31.** nest
papużka	**15.** parakeet		dudek	**32.** roadrunner

A

B

Ryby	**A. Fish**
konik morski	**1.** sea horse
pstrąg	**2.** trout
miecznik	**3.** swordfish
ogon	**a.** tail
płetwa	**b.** fin
skrzela	**c.** gill
węgorz	**4.** eel
rekin	**5.** shark
płaszczka, trygon	**6.** stingray
flądra	**7.** flounder

Płazy i gady	**B. Amphibians and Reptiles**
aligator	**8.** alligator
wąż (prążkowany)	**9.** (garter) snake
grzechotnik	**10.** rattlesnake
kobra	**11.** cobra
żółw morski	**12.** turtle
iguana	**13.** iguana
salamandra	**14.** salamander
jaszczurka	**15.** lizard
kijanka	**16.** tadpole
żaba	**17.** frog
żółw	**18.** tortoise
tarcza, skorupa	**a.** shell

Torbacze, ssaki bezzębne lub latające

Pouched, Toothless, or Flying Mammals

koala — **1.** koala
pancernik — **2.** armadillo
kangur — **3.** kangaroo
ogon — **a.** tail
kończyny tylne — **b.** hind legs
torba — **c.** pouch
kończyny przednie — **d.** forelegs
nietoperz — **4.** bat
mrówkojad — **5.** anteater

Gryzonie

Rodents

wiewiórka ziemna — **6.** chipmunk
szczur — **7.** rat
suseł — **8.** gopher
mysz — **9.** mouse

wiewiórka — **10.** squirrel
jeżozwierz — **11.** porcupine
kolec — **a.** quill
bóbr — **12.** beaver
królik — **13.** rabbit

Ssaki kopytne

Hoofed Mammals

hipopotam — **14.** hippopotamus
lama — **15.** llama
nosorożec — **16.** rhinoceros
róg — **a.** horn
słoń — **17.** elephant
trąba — **a.** trunk
kieł — **b.** tusk
zebra — **18.** zebra

bizon	**19.** bison	żyrafa	**29.** giraffe
kucyk	**20.** pony	wieprz, świnia	**30.** hog
koń	**21.** horse	cielę	**31.** calf
grzywa	**a.** mane	krowa	**32.** cow
źrebię	**22.** foal	wielbłąd	**33.** camel
osioł	**23.** donkey	garb	**a.** hump
jagnię	**24.** lamb	byk	**34.** bull
owca	**25.** sheep	łoś amerykański	**35.** moose
jeleń, zwierzyna płowa	**26.** deer	łopata	**a.** antler
młode	**27.** fawn	kopyto	**b.** hoof
koza	**28.** goat		

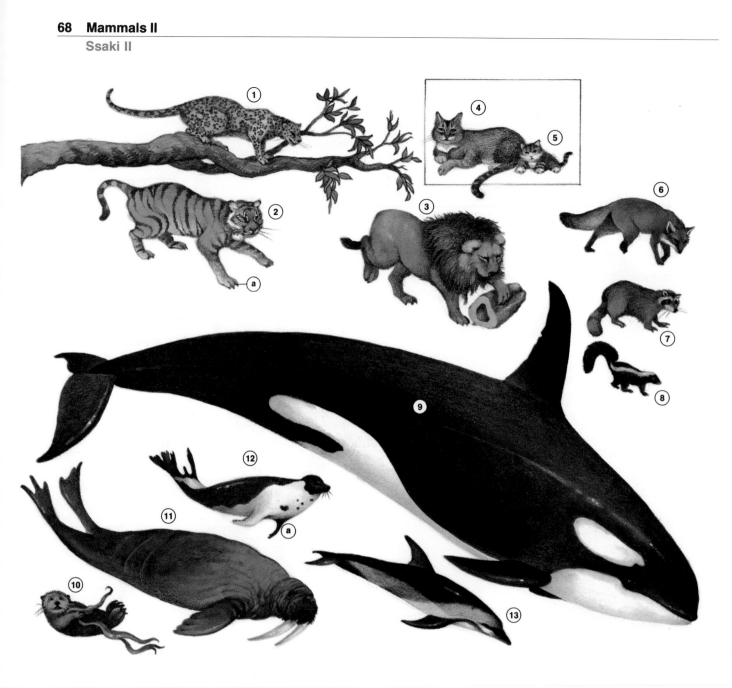

lampart	**1.** leopard		**Ssaki wodne**	**Aquatic Mammals**
tygrys	**2.** tiger		wieloryb	**9.** whale
pazur	**a.** claw		wydra	**10.** otter
lew	**3.** lion		mors	**11.** walrus
kot	**4.** cat		foka	**12.** seal
kociak	**5.** kitten		płetwa	**a.** flipper
lis	**6.** fox		delfin	**13.** dolphin
szop	**7.** raccoon			
skunks	**8.** skunk			

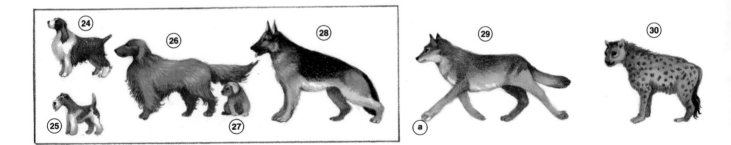

Naczelne	**Primates**
małpa	**14.** monkey
gibon	**15.** gibbon
szympans	**16.** chimpanzee
goryl	**17.** gorilla
orangutan	**18.** orangutan
pawian	**19.** baboon
Niedźwiedzie	**Bears**
panda	**20.** panda
niedźwiedź czarny	**21.** black bear
niedźwiedź polarny	**22.** polar bear
niedźwiedź północnoamerykański	**23.** grizzly bear

Psy	**Dogs**
spaniel	**24.** spaniel
terier	**25.** terrier
pies myśliwski	**26.** retriever
szczeniak	**27.** puppy
owczarek	**28.** shepherd
wilk	**29.** wolf
pazur	**a.** paw
hiena	**30.** hyena

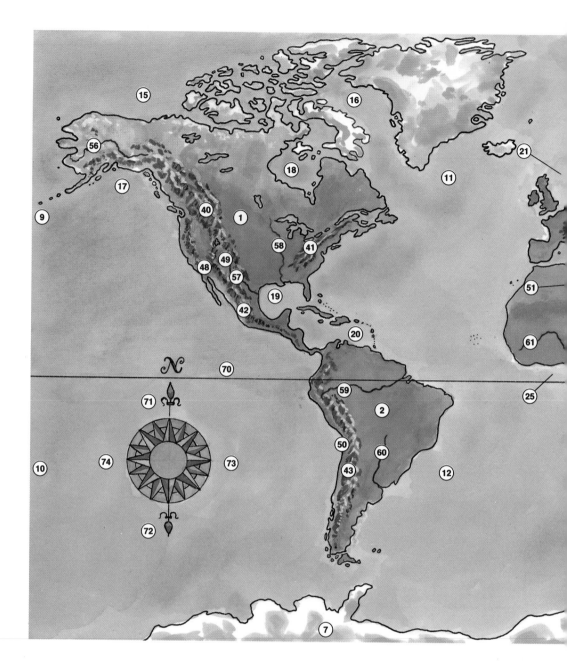

Kontynenty	**Continents**		Ocean Indyjski	**13.** Indian		Morze Czarne	**26.** Black Sea
Ameryka Północna	**1.** North America		Basen Antarktyczny	**14.** Antarctic		Morze Kaspijskie	**27.** Caspian Sea
Ameryka Południowa	**2.** South America					Zatoka Perska	**28.** Persian Gulf
Europa	**3.** Europe		**Morza i zatoki**		**Seas, Gulfs, and Bays**	Morze Czerwone	**29.** Red Sea
Afryka	**4.** Africa		Morze Beauforta	**15.** Beaufort Sea		Morze Arabskie	**30.** Arabian Sea
Azja	**5.** Asia		Morze Baffina	**16.** Baffin Bay		Morze Karskie	**31.** Kara Sea
Australia	**6.** Australia		Zatoka Alaska	**17.** Gulf of Alaska		Zatoka Bengalska	**32.** Bay of Bengal
Antarktyda	**7.** Antarctica		Zatoka Hudsona	**18.** Hudson Bay		Morze Łaptiewów	**33.** Laptev Sea
			Zatoka Meksykańska	**19.** Gulf of Mexico		Morze Beringa	**34.** Bering Sea
Oceany	**Oceans**		Morze Karaibskie	**20.** Caribbean Sea		Morze Ochockie	**35.** Sea of Okhotsk
Ocean Lodowaty	**8.** Arctic		Morze Północne	**21.** North Sea		Morze Japońskie	**36.** Sea of Japan
Północny Pacyfik	**9.** North Pacific		Morze Bałtyckie	**22.** Baltic Sea		Morze Żółte	**37.** Yellow Sea
Południowy Pacyfik	**10.** South Pacific		Morze Barentsa	**23.** Barents Sea		Morze Wschodniochińskie	**38.** East China Sea
Północny Atlantyk	**11.** North Atlantic		Morze Śródziemne	**24.** Mediterranean Sea		Morze Południowochińskie	**39.** South China Sea
Południowy Atlantyk	**12.** South Atlantic		Zatoka Gwinejska	**25.** Gulf of Guinea			

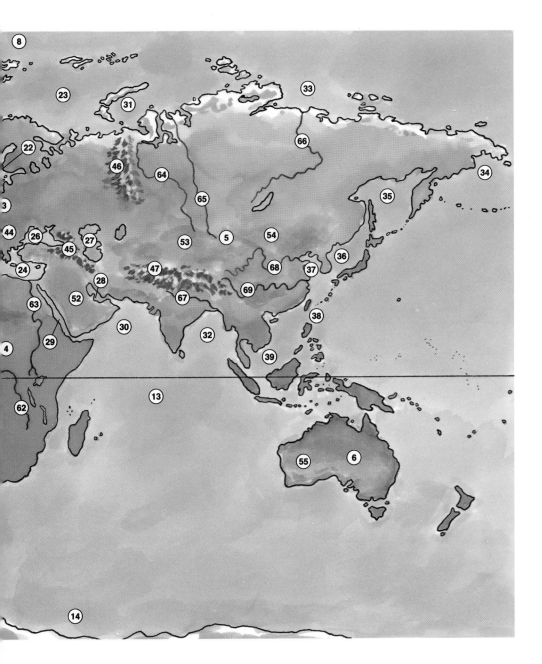

Łańcuchy górskie	**Mountain Ranges**	Pustynia Takla Makan	**53.** Takla Makan	Lena	**66.** Lena
Góry Skaliste	**40.** Rocky Mountains	Pustynia Gobi	**54.** Gobi	Ganges	**67.** Ganges
Appalachy	**41.** Appalachian Mountains	Wielka Pustynia Piaszczysta	**55.** Great Sandy	Huanghe	**68.** Huang
Sierra Madre	**42.** Sierra Madre			Jangcy	**69.** Yangtze
Andy	**43.** Andes	**Rzeki**	**Rivers**		
Alpy	**44.** Alps	Jukon	**56.** Yukon	równik	**70.** equator
Kaukaz	**45.** Caucasus	Rio Grande	**57.** Rio Grande	północ	**71.** north
Ural	**46.** Urals	Missisipi	**58.** Mississippi	południe	**72.** south
Himalaje	**47.** Himalayas	Amazonka	**59.** Amazon	wschód	**73.** east
		Parana	**60.** Paraná	zachód	**74.** west
Pustynie	**Deserts**	Niger	**61.** Niger		
Pustynia Mojave	**48.** Mojave	Kongo	**62.** Congo		
Pustynia Painted	**49.** Painted	Nil	**63.** Nile		
Pustynia Atakama	**50.** Atacama	Ob	**64.** Ob		
Sahara	**51.** Sahara	Jenisej	**65.** Yenisey		
Pustynia Rub al-Chali	**52.** Rub' al Khali				

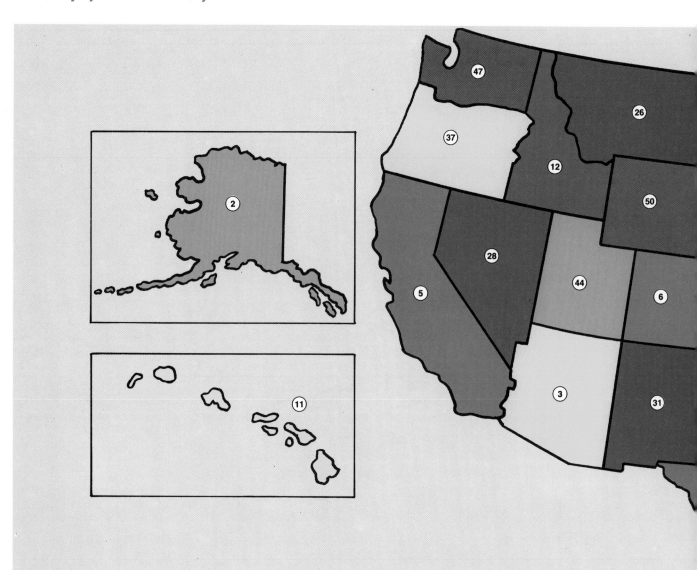

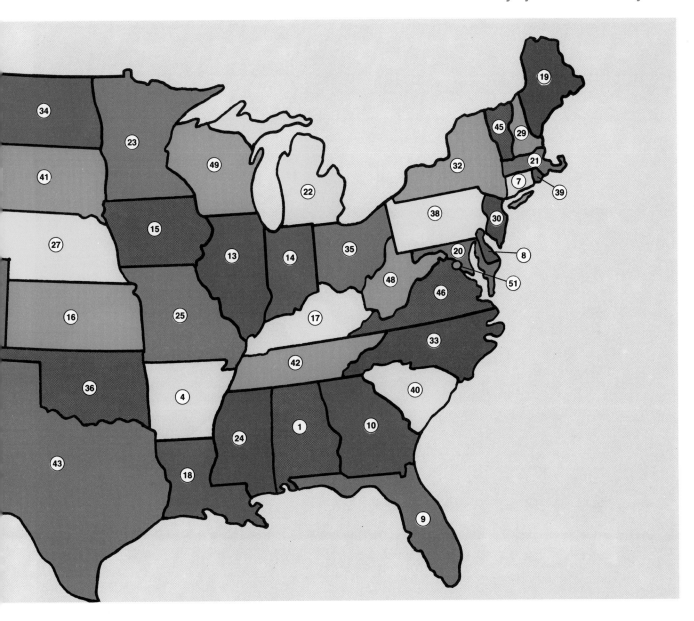

Missouri	**25.** Missouri	Karolina Południowa	**40.** South Carolina
Montana	**26.** Montana	Dakota Południowa	**41.** South Dakota
Nebraska	**27.** Nebraska	Tennessee	**42.** Tennessee
Nevada	**28.** Nevada	Teksas	**43.** Texas
New Hampshire	**29.** New Hampshire	Utah	**44.** Utah
New Jersey	**30.** New Jersey	Vermont	**45.** Vermont
Nowy Meksyk	**31.** New Mexico	Wirginia	**46.** Virginia
Nowy Jork	**32.** New York	Waszyngton	**47.** Washington
Karolina Północna	**33.** North Carolina	Wirginia Zachodnia	**48.** West Virginia
Dakota Północna	**34.** North Dakota	Wisconsin	**49.** Wisconsin
Ohio	**35.** Ohio	Wyoming	**50.** Wyoming
Oklahoma	**36.** Oklahoma		
Oregon	**37.** Oregon	Dystrykt Kolumbii	**51.** District of Columbia
Pensylwania	**38.** Pennsylvania		
Rhode Island	**39.** Rhode Island		

Przestrzeń kosmiczna | **A. Outer Space**
galaktyka | **1.** galaxy
kometa | **2.** comet
konstelacja (Wielki Wóz) | **3.** (Big Dipper) constellation
gwiazda | **4.** star
meteor | **5.** meteor

Układ słoneczny | **B. The Solar System**
zaćmienie Księżyca | **6.** lunar eclipse
Słońce | **7.** Sun
Ziemia | **8.** Earth
Księżyc | **9.** Moon
zaćmienie Słońca | **10.** solar eclipse

Planety | *The Planets*
Merkury | **11.** Mercury
Wenus | **12.** Venus
Ziemia | **13.** Earth

Mars | **14.** Mars
Jowisz | **15.** Jupiter
Saturn | **16.** Saturn
pierścień | **a.** ring
Uran | **17.** Uranus
Neptun | **18.** Neptune
Pluton | **19.** Pluto
asteroida, planetoida | **20.** asteroid
orbita | **21.** orbit
teleskop | **22.** telescope

Fazy Księżyca | **C. Phases of the Moon**
pierwsza kwadra | **23.** first quarter
pełnia Księżyca | **24.** full moon
ostatnia kwadra | **25.** last quarter
nów | **26.** new moon

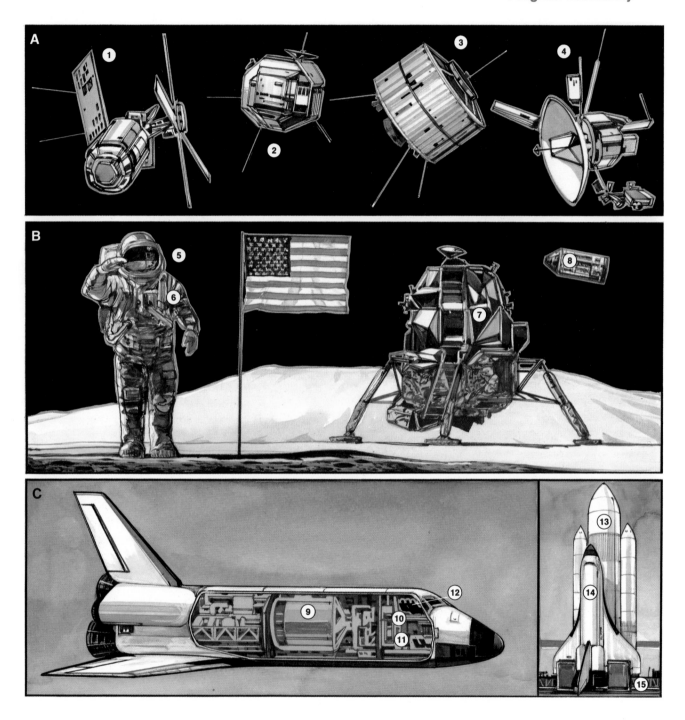

Statek kosmiczny | **A. Spacecraft**
stacja kosmiczna | **1.** space station
satelita komunikacyjny | **2.** communication satellite
satelita meteorologiczny | **3.** weather satellite
sonda kosmiczna | **4.** space probe

Lądowanie na Księżycu | **B. Landing on the Moon**
astronauta | **5.** astronaut
skafander kosmiczny | **6.** space suit
lądownik | **7.** lunar module
moduł dowodzenia | **8.** command module

Prom kosmiczny | **C. The Space Shuttle**
ładownia | **9.** cargo bay
pomost kontroli lotu | **10.** flight deck
pomieszczenia dla załogi | **11.** living quarters
załoga | **12.** crew
rakieta | **13.** rocket
wahadłowiec | **14.** space shuttle
wyrzutnia | **15.** launchpad

Klasa, sala szkolna

flaga	**1.** flag
zegar	**2.** clock
głośnik	**3.** loudspeaker
nauczyciel	**4.** teacher
tablica	**5.** chalkboard
szafka	**6.** locker
tablica ogłoszeń	**7.** bulletin board
komputer	**8.** computer
tacka na kredę	**9.** chalk tray
kreda	**10.** chalk
zmywacz, gąbka	**11.** eraser
hall	**12.** hall
wkład do skoroszytu	**13.** (loose-leaf) paper
skoroszyt	**14.** ring binder

kołonotatnik	**15.** spiral notebook
ławka	**16.** desk
klej	**17.** glue
pędzelek	**18.** brush
uczeń	**19.** student
temperówka	**20.** pencil sharpener
gumka do ołówka	**21.** pencil eraser
długopis	**22.** ballpoint pen
linijka	**23.** ruler
ołówek	**24.** pencil
pinezka	**25.** thumbtack
podręcznik	**26.** (text)book
rzutnik pisma	**27.** overhead projector

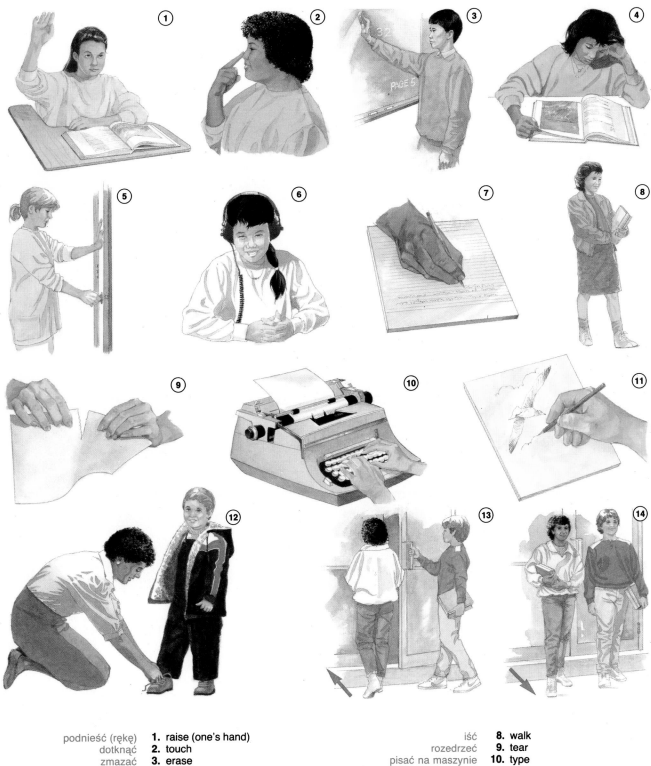

podnieść (rękę)	**1.** raise (one's hand)	iść	**8.** walk
dotknąć	**2.** touch	rozedrzeć	**9.** tear
zmazać	**3.** erase	pisać na maszynie	**10.** type
czytać	**4.** read	rysować	**11.** draw
zamknąć	**5.** close	wiązać	**12.** tie
słuchać	**6.** listen	wychodzić	**13.** leave
pisać	**7.** write	wchodzić	**14.** enter

Laboratorium fizyczno-chemiczne

pryzmat	**1. prism**	statyw z pierścieniem	**19. ring stand**
kolba	**2. flask**	palnik Bunsena	**20. Bunsen burner**
płytka Petriego	**3. petri dish**	płomień	**21. flame**
waga	**4. scale**	termometr	**22. thermometer**
odważnik	**5. weights**	zlewka	**23. beaker**
siatka druciana	**6. wire mesh screen**	stół	**24. bench**
zacisk	**7. clamp**	menzurka	**25. graduated cylinder**
stojak	**8. rack**	zakraplacz	**26. medicine dropper**
probówka	**9. test tube**	magnes	**27. magnet**
korek	**10. stopper**	kleszcze	**28. forceps**
papier milimetrowy	**11. graph paper**	szczypce	**29. tongs**
okulary ochronne	**12. safety glasses**	mikroskop	**30. microscope**
minutnik	**13. timer**	szkiełko	**31. slide**
pipeta	**14. pipette**	pinceta	**32. tweezers**
szkło powiększające	**15. magnifying glass**	zestaw do preparowania	**33. dissection kit**
filtr papierowy	**16. filter paper**	stołek	**34. stool**
lejek	**17. funnel**		
rura gumowa	**18. rubber tubing**		

A

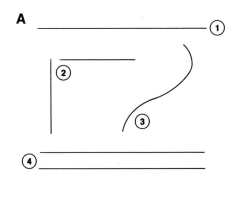

B

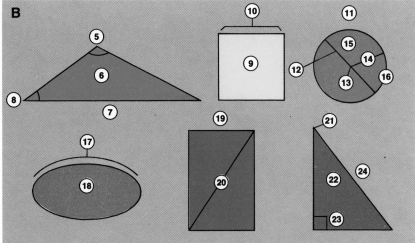

C

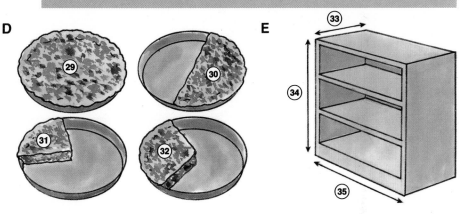

D

E

Linie	**A. Lines**
linia prosta	**1.** straight line
linie prostopadłe	**2.** perpendicular lines
krzywa	**3.** curve
linie równoległe	**4.** parallel lines

Figury geometryczne	**B. Geometrical Figures**
kąt rozwarty	**5.** obtuse angle
trójkąt	**6.** triangle
podstawa	**7.** base
kąt ostry	**8.** acute angle
kwadrat	**9.** square
bok	**10.** side
koło	**11.** circle
średnica	**12.** diameter
środek	**13.** center
promień	**14.** radius
część koła	**15.** section
łuk	**16.** arc
obwód	**17.** circumference
elipsa	**18.** oval
prostokąt	**19.** rectangle
przekątna	**20.** diagonal
wierzchołek	**21.** apex

trójkąt prostokątny	**22.** right triangle
kąt prosty	**23.** right angle
przeciwprostokątna	**24.** hypotenuse

Bryły	**C. Solid Figures**
ostrosłup	**25.** pyramid
walec	**26.** cylinder
sześcian	**27.** cube
stożek	**28.** cone

Ułamki	**D. Fractions**
całość	**29.** whole
połówka	**30.** a half (1/2)
ćwiartka	**31.** a quarter (1/4)
trzecia część	**32.** a third (1/3)

Wymiary	**E. Measurement**
głębokość	**33.** depth
wysokość	**34.** height
szerokość	**35.** width
długość	**36.** length

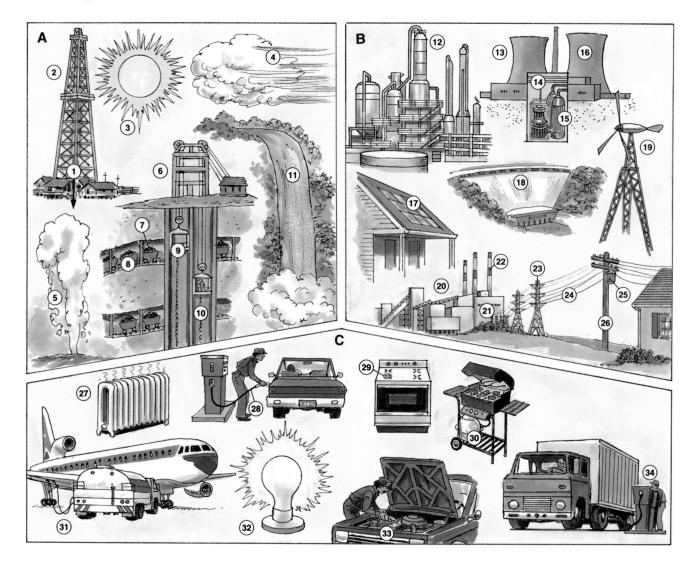

Żródła energii	A. Sources of Power
szyb naftowy	1. oil well
wieża wiertnicza	2. derrick
słońce	3. sun
wiatr	4. wind
gejzer	5. geyser
kopalnia węgla	6. coal mine
węgiel	7. coal
wagonik	8. shuttle car
winda	9. elevator
szyb	10. shaft
wodospad	11. waterfall

Wytwarzanie energii	B. Generation of Power
rafineria	12. refinery
reaktor atomowy	13. nuclear reactor
rdzeń	14. core
pręty uranowe	15. uranium rods
wieża chłodząca	16. cooling tower
kolektor słoneczny	17. solar collector

zapora	18. dam
wiatrak	19. windmill
elektrownia	20. power station
generator prądu	21. electrical generator
komin	22. smokestack
słupy wysokiego napięcia	23. transmission towers
linie elektryczne	24. power lines
transformator	25. transformer
słup energetyczny	26. utility pole

Użycie i produkty	C. Uses and Products
ciepło	27. heat
benzyna	28. gas(oline)
gaz ziemny	29. natural gas
propan	30. propane gas
paliwo do silników odrzutowych	31. jet fuel
elektryczność	32. electricity
olej silnikowy	33. motor oil
olej napędowy	34. diesel fuel

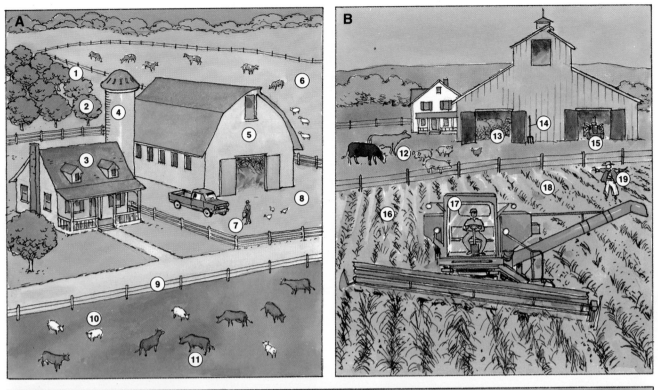

Gospodarstwo mleczne	**A. Dairy Farm**		siano (w beli)	**13.** (bale of) hay
sad	**1.** orchard		widły	**14.** pitchfork
drzewo owocowe	**2.** fruit tree		traktor	**15.** tractor
dom mieszkalny	**3.** farmhouse		pole (pszenicy)	**16.** (wheat) field
silos	**4.** silo		kombajn	**17.** combine
stodoła	**5.** barn		zagon, grządka	**18.** row
pastwisko	**6.** pasture		strach na wróble	**19.** scarecrow
farmer, rolnik	**7.** farmer			
podwórko	**8.** barnyard		**Gospodarstwo hodowlane**	**C. Ranch**
płot	**9.** fence		bydło (w stadzie)	**20.** (herd of) cattle
owce	**10.** sheep		kowboj	**21.** cowboy
krowy mleczne	**11.** dairy cow		dziewczyna—kowboj	**22.** cowgirl
			konie	**23.** horses
Gospodarstwo rolne	**B. Wheat Farm**		zagroda	**24.** corral
inwentarz	**12.** livestock		koryto	**25.** trough

Plac budowy	A. Construction Site		deska	16. board
krokwie	1. rafters		mierniczy	17. linesman
dachówka	2. shingle		wysięgnik z gondolą	18. cherry picker
poziomica	3. level			
kask roboczy	4. hard hat		Roboty drogowe	B. Road Work
budowniczy, majster	5. builder		pachołek	19. cone
plany, rysunki techniczne	6. blueprints		chorągiewka	20. flag
rusztowanie	7. scaffolding		zapora	21. barricade
drabina	8. ladder		młot pneumatyczny	22. jackhammer
szczebel	9. rung		taczka	23. wheelbarrow
cement	10. cement		bariera środkowa	24. center divider
fundament	11. foundation		betoniarka	25. cement mixer
cegły	12. bricks		koparka	26. backhoe
kilof	13. pickax		spychacz	27. bulldozer
robotnik budowlany	14. construction worker			
szufla	15. shovel			

telefonistka	**1.** switchboard operator	komputer	**16.** computer
słuchawki z mikrofonem	**2.** headset	fotel biurowy	**17.** typing chair
łącznica telefoniczna	**3.** switchboard	kierownik	**18.** manager
drukarka	**4.** printer	kalkulator	**19.** calculator
pomieszczenie biurowe	**5.** cubicle	półka na książki	**20.** bookcase
maszynistka	**6.** typist	segregator szufladowy	**21.** file cabinet
edytor tekstu	**7.** word processor	teczka na akta	**22.** file folder
wydruk	**8.** printout	archiwista	**23.** file clerk
kalendarz	**9.** calendar	kopiarka	**24.** photocopier
maszyna do pisania	**10.** typewriter	notatnik służbowy	**25.** message pad
sekretarka	**11.** secretary	blok do pisania (pism prawniczych)	**26.** (legal) pad
pisma przychodzące	**12.** in-box	zszywacz	**27.** stapler
biurko	**13.** desk	spinacz	**28.** paper clips
indeks adresowy	**14.** rolodex	przyrząd do usuwania zszywek	**29.** staple remover
telefon	**15.** telephone	temperówka	**30.** pencil sharpener
		koperta	**31.** envelope

aptekarz	**1.** pharmacist
mechanik samochodowy	**2.** mechanic
fryzjer męski	**3.** barber
biuro podróży	**4.** travel agent
elektrotechnik	**5.** repairperson
krawiec	**6.** tailor
sprzedawca warzyw	**7.** greengrocer

piekarz	**8.** baker
optyk	**9.** optician
fryzjer damski	**10.** hairdresser
kwiaciarz	**11.** florist
jubiler	**12.** jeweller
rzeźnik	**13.** butcher

Naprawy i konserwacja	**A. Repair and Maintenance**	Służba domowa	**B. Household Services**
hydraulik	**1.** plumber	pomoc domowa	**8.** housekeeper
stolarz	**2.** carpenter	dozorca	**9.** janitor
ogrodnik	**3.** gardener	goniec, dostawca	**10.** delivery boy
ślusarz	**4.** locksmith	odźwierny	**11.** doorman
pośrednik w handlu nieruchomościami	**5.** real estate agent		
elektryk	**6.** electrician	Praca w fabryce	**C. Factory Work**
malarz	**7.** painter	robotnik	**12.** shop worker
		brygadzista	**13.** foreman

Środki przekazu i sztuka	A. Media and Arts
meteorolog	1. weather forecaster
prezenter dziennika	2. newscaster
artysta plastyk	3. artist
fotograf	4. photographer
modelka	5. model
projektant mody	6. fashion designer
pisarz, autor	7. writer
architekt	8. architect
disc jockey	9. disc jockey (DJ)
kamerzysta	10. cameraperson

reporter	11. reporter
sprzedawca	12. salesperson
Bankowość	**B. Banking**
kontroler	13. officer
strażnik	14. security guard
kasjer	15. teller
Pracownicy biznesu	**C. Business Workers**
programista komputerowy	16. computer programmer
recepcjonistka	17. receptionist
księgowy	18. accountant
goniec	19. messenger

zoo	1. zoo
muszla koncertowa	2. band shell
sprzedawca uliczny	3. vendor
wózek ręczny	4. hand truck
karuzela	5. merry-go-round
jeździec na koniu	6. horseback rider
ścieżka do jazdy na koniu	7. bridle path
sadzawka (dla kaczek)	8. (duck) pond
alejka dla biegaczy	9. jogging path
ławka	10. bench
kosz na śmieci	11. trash can
zjeżdżalnia	12. slide
piaskownica	13. sandbox
fontanna	14. sprinkler
plac zabaw	15. playground
huśtawki krzesełkowe	16. swings
tor przeszkód	17. jungle gym
huśtawka na desce	18. seesaw
źródełko, woda do picia	19. water fountain

płaskowyż	**1.** plateau	podbierak	**9.** fishing net
turyści piesi	**2.** hikers	wysokie buty nieprzemakalne	**10.** waders
kanion	**3.** canyon	skałki	**11.** rocks
wzgórza	**4.** hill		
strażnik parku	**5.** park ranger	**Miejsce biwakowe**	**Picnic Area**
		grill	**12.** grill
Wędkarstwo	**Fishing**	koszyk	**13.** picnic basket
strumień	**6.** stream	termos	**14.** thermos
wędka	**7.** fishing rod	stół na piknik	**15.** picnic table
żyłka	**8.** fishing line		

Spływ tratwą	**Rafting**		Obozowisko	**Camping**
tratwa	**16.** raft		namiot	**24.** tent
bystrza	**17.** rapids		kuchenka	**25.** camp stove
wodospad	**18.** waterfall		śpiwór	**26.** sleeping bag
			wyposażenie	**27.** gear
Wspinaczka wysokogórska	**Mountain Climbing**		plecak ze stelażem	**28.** frame backpack
góra	**19.** mountain		latarnia	**29.** lantern
szczyt	**20.** peak		śledź	**30.** stake
skała	**21.** cliff		ognisko obozowe	**31.** campfire
uprząż	**22.** harness		lasy	**32.** woods
lina	**23.** rope			

chodnik z desek	**1.** boardwalk		wydmy	**12.** sand dunes
bufet	**2.** refreshment stand		frisbi	**13.** Frisbee ™
motel	**3.** motel		okulary słoneczne	**14.** sunglasses
rowerzysta	**4.** biker		ręcznik kąpielowy	**15.** beach towel
gwizdek	**5.** whistle		wiaderko	**16.** pail
ratownik	**6.** lifeguard		łopatka	**17.** shovel
lornetka	**7.** binoculars		kostium kąpielowy	**18.** bathing suit
krzesło ratownika	**8.** lifeguard chair		opalający się	**19.** sunbather
koło ratunkowe	**9.** life preserver		leżak	**20.** beach chair
łódź ratunkowa	**10.** lifeboat		parasol plażowy	**21.** beach umbrella
piłka plażowa	**11.** beach ball			

latawiec	**22.** kite		zamek z piasku	**32.** sandcastle
biegacze	**23.** runners		kąpielówki	**33.** bathing trunks
fala	**24.** wave		fajka	**34.** snorkel
deska surfingowa	**25.** surfboard		maska	**35.** mask
materac nadmuchiwany	**26.** air mattress		płetwy	**36.** flippers
deska treningowa	**27.** kickboard		butla z powietrzem	**37.** scuba tank
pływak	**28.** swimmer		pianka	**38.** wet suit
dętka	**29.** tube		olejek do opalania	**39.** suntan lotion
woda	**30.** water		muszla	**40.** shell
piasek	**31.** sand		lodówka turystyczna	**41.** cooler

Gry zespołowe

Baseball	**Baseball**		Lacrosse	**Lacrosse**
sędzia	**1.** umpire		maska	**15.** face guard
zawodnik chwytający (łapacz)	**2.** catcher		rakieta	**16.** lacrosse stick
maska	**3.** catcher's mask			
rękawica	**4.** catcher's mitt		**Hokej na lodzie**	**Ice Hockey**
pałka	**5.** bat		krążek	**17.** puck
kask zawodnika odbijającego	**6.** batting helmet		kij hokejowy	**18.** hockey stick
zawodnik odbijający	**7.** batter			
			Koszykówka	**Basketball**
Baseball—mała liga	**Little League Baseball**		tablica	**19.** backboard
zawodnik małej ligi	**8.** Little Leaguer		kosz	**20.** basket
strój	**9.** uniform		piłka do koszykówki	**21.** basketball
Softball	**Softball**		**Siatkówka**	**Volleyball**
piłka miękka	**10.** softball		piłka do siatkówki	**22.** volleyball
czapka	**11.** cap		siatka	**23.** net
rękawica	**12.** glove			
			Piłka nożna	**Soccer**
Football amerykański	**Football**		bramkarz	**24.** goalie
piłka	**13.** football		bramka	**25.** goal
kask	**14.** helmet		piłka nożna	**26.** soccer ball

Diament baseballowy	**A. Baseball Diamond**	Pole footballowe	**B. Football Field**
lewy gracz w polu	**1.** left fielder	tablica wyników	**19.** scoreboard
środkowy gracz w polu	**2.** center fielder	wodzireje	**20.** cheerleaders
prawy gracz w polu	**3.** right fielder	trener	**21.** coach
gracz przy trzeciej bazie	**4.** third baseman	sędzia	**22.** referee
gracz łapiący krótkie odbicia	**5.** shortstop	pole punktowe	**23.** end zone
baza	**6.** base	napastnik skrzydłowy	**24.** split end
gracz przy drugiej bazie	**7.** second baseman	lewy przechwytujący	**25.** left tackle
gracz przy pierwszej bazie	**8.** first baseman	lewy osłaniający	**26.** left guard
linia autowa	**9.** foul line	środkowy osłaniający	**27.** center
trybuny	**10.** stands	prawy osłaniający	**28.** right guard
kopczyk miotacza	**11.** pitcher's mound	prawy przechwytujący	**29.** right tackle
zawodnik miotający	**12.** pitcher	napastnik skrzydłowy (bliższy)	**30.** tight end
pomieszczenie dla drużyn	**13.** dugout	napastnik flankujący	**31.** flanker
zawodnik odbijający (pałkarz)	**14.** batter	napastnik środkowy	**32.** quarterback
baza-meta	**15.** home plate	napastnik dalszy	**33.** halfback
łapacz	**16.** catcher	napastnik cofnięty	**34.** fullback
sędzia	**17.** umpire	słup bramkowy	**35.** goalpost
chłopiec podający pałki	**18.** batboy		

Sporty indywidualne

Tenis		**Tennis**
piłka tenisowa	**1.**	tennis ball
rakieta	**2.**	racket

Bowling		**Bowling**
rynna	**3.**	gutter
tor	**4.**	lane
kręgle	**5.**	pin
kula	**6.**	bowling ball

Golf		**Golf**
piłeczka golfowa	**7.**	golf ball
dołek	**8.**	hole
kij do umieszczania piłeczki w dołku	**9.**	putter
zawodnik grający w golfa	**10.**	golfer

Piłeczka ręczna		**Handball**
rękawica	**11.**	glove
piłeczka	**12.**	handball
kort	**13.**	court

Boks		**Boxing**
ochraniacz na głowę	**14.**	head protector
rękawica	**15.**	glove
sędzia	**16.**	referee
ring	**17.**	ring

Tenis stołowy		**Ping-Pong**
paletka	**18.**	paddle
piłeczka ping pongowa	**19.**	ping-pong ball

Wyścigi konne		**Horse Racing**
siodło	**20.**	saddle
dżokej	**21.**	jockey
wodze	**22.**	reins

Gimnastyka		**Gymnastics**
gimnastyczka	**23.**	gymnast
równoważnia	**24.**	balance beam

Jazda na łyżwach		**Ice Skating**
tor	**25.**	rink
łyżwa	**26.**	skate
ostrze	**27.**	blade

Racquetball		**Racquetball**
okulary ochronne	**28.**	safety goggles
rakieta	**29.**	racquet
piłka	**30.**	racquetball

Lekkoatletyka		**Track and Field**
biegacz	**31.**	runner
bieżnia	**32.**	track

Narciarstwo biegowe		**Cross-Country Skiing**
narty	**33.**	skis
kijek	**34.**	pole
narciarz	**35.**	skier

Kort tenisowy	**A. Tennis Court**		Zbocze narciarskie	**C. Ski Slope**
pole serwisowe	**1.** service court		kijek	**14.** pole
siatka	**2.** net		but narciarski	**15.** ski boot
linia serwisowa	**3.** service line		wiązanie	**16.** binding
linia główna	**4.** baseline		narta	**17.** ski
			wyciąg narciarski	**18.** ski lift
Tor golfowy	**B. Golf Course**			
kije	**5.** clubs		Tor wyścigowy	**D. Race Track**
przeszkoda	**6.** rough		dystans, tor	**19.** stretch
torba golfowa	**7.** golf bag		maszyna startowa	**20.** starting gate
wózek golfowy	**8.** golf cart		celownik	**21.** finish line
flaga	**9.** flag			
trawnik	**10.** green			
pułapka piaskowa	**11.** sand trap			
tor	**12.** fairway			
kołek	**13.** tee			

Czasowniki związane ze sportem

uderzać	**1.** hit	podawać	**5.** pass
serwować	**2.** serve	biec	**6.** run
kopać	**3.** kick	padać	**7.** fall
łapać	**4.** catch	skakać	**8.** jump

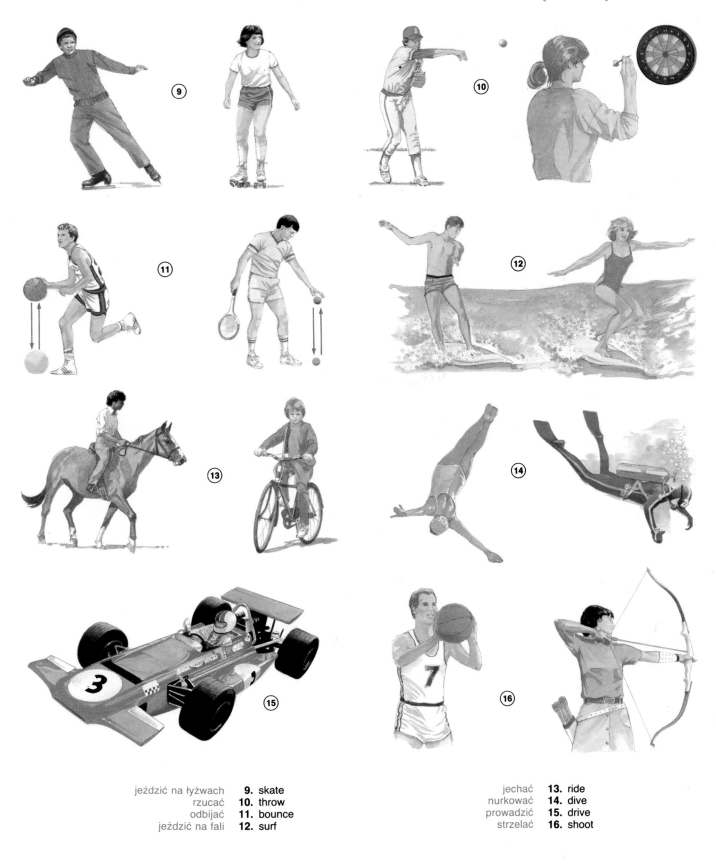

jeździć na łyżwach	**9.**	skate
rzucać	**10.**	throw
odbijać	**11.**	bounce
jeździć na fali	**12.**	surf

jechać	**13.**	ride
nurkować	**14.**	dive
prowadzić	**15.**	drive
strzelać	**16.**	shoot

Strunowe	**Strings**		Instrumenty perkusyjne	**Percussion**
fortepian	**1.** piano		tamburyn	**17.** tambourine
klawiatura	**a.** keyboard		czynele	**18.** cymbals
nuty	**2.** sheet music		bęben	**19.** drum
ukulele	**3.** ukulele		pałeczki	**a.** drumsticks
mandolina	**4.** mandolin		konga	**20.** conga
banjo	**5.** banjo		kocioł	**21.** kettledrum
harfa	**6.** harp		bongosy	**22.** bongos
skrzypce	**7.** violin			
smyczek	**a.** bow		**Instrumenty blaszane**	**Brass**
altówka	**8.** viola		puzon	**23.** trombone
wiolonczela	**9.** cello		saksofon	**24.** saxophone
kontrabas	**10.** bass		trąbka	**25.** trumpet
struna	**a.** string		rożek angielski	**26.** French horn
gitara	**11.** guitar		tuba	**27.** tuba
kostka	**a.** pick			
			Inne instrumenty	**Other Instruments**
Drewniane instrumenty dęte	**Woodwinds**		akordeon	**28.** accordion
piccolo	**12.** piccolo		organy	**29.** organ
flet	**13.** flute		harmonijka ustna	**30.** harmonica
fagot	**14.** bassoon		ksylofon	**31.** xylophone
obój	**15.** oboe			
klarnet	**16.** clarinet			

Balet	**A. The Ballet**
kurtyna	**1.** curtain
dekoracje	**2.** scenery
tancerz	**3.** dancer
reflektor punktowy	**4.** spotlight
scena	**5.** stage
orkiestra	**6.** orchestra
podium	**7.** podium
dyrygent	**8.** conductor
batuta	**9.** baton
muzyk	**10.** musician
loża	**11.** box seat
fotele parteru	**12.** orchestra seating
międzypiętrze, antresola	**13.** mezzanine
balkon	**14.** balcony
publiczność	**15.** audience
bileter	**16.** usher
programy	**17.** programs

Komedia muzyczna	**B. Musical Comedy**
chór	**18.** chorus
aktor	**19.** actor
aktorka	**20.** actress

Grupa rockowa	**C. Rock Group**
syntetyzator	**21.** synthesizer
muzyk grający na klawiaturach	**22.** keyboard player
gitarzysta basowy	**23.** bass guitarist
wokalistka	**24.** singer
gitarzysta prowadzący	**25.** lead guitarist
gitara elektryczna	**26.** electric guitar
perkusista	**27.** drummer

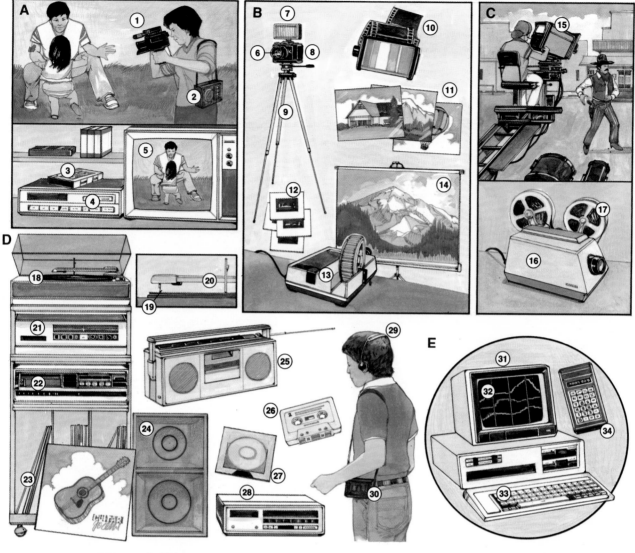

Wideo	A. **Video**
kamera wideo	**1.** video camera
Minicam™	**2.** Minicam ™
kaseta wideo (taśma)	**3.** videocassette (tape)
magnetowid	**4.** VCR (videocassette recorder)
telewizor	**5.** television

Fotografia	B. **Photography**
obiektyw	**6.** lens
lampa błyskowa	**7.** flash
aparat	**8.** camera
statyw	**9.** tripod
film (w rolce)	**10.** (roll of) film
odbitki	**11.** prints
przezrocza	**12.** slides
rzutnik przezroczy	**13.** slide projector
ekran	**14.** screen

Film	C. **Film**
kamera filmowa	**15.** movie camera
projektor	**16.** projector
film (na szpuli)	**17.** (reel of) film

Sprzęt foniczny	D. **Audio**
adapter	**18.** turntable
igła zespolona	**19.** cartridge needle
ramię	**20.** arm
odbiornik	**21.** receiver
deck kasetowy	**22.** cassette deck
płyty	**23.** records
głośniki	**24.** speaker
stereofoniczny magnetofon kasetowy	**25.** stereo cassette player
kaseta	**26.** cassette
płyta kompaktowa	**27.** compact disc (CD)
odtwarzacz płyt kompaktowych	**28.** compact disc player
słuchawki	**29.** headphones
walkman firmy Sony	**30.** Sony Walkman

Komputery	E. **Computers**
komputer osobisty	**31.** personal computer (PC)
monitor	**32.** monitor
klawiatura	**33.** keyboard
kalkulator	**34.** calculator

Szycie	**A. Sewing**	ścieg	**19.** stitch
maszyna do szycia	**1.** sewing machine	szpilka	**20.** pin
(szpulka) nici	**2.** (spool of) thread	naparstek	**21.** thimble
poduszka do igieł	**3.** pincushion		
materiał	**4.** material	Inne robótki z użyciem igły	**B. Other Needlecrafts**
nożyczki z ząbkami	**5.** pinking shears	robótka na drutach	**22.** knitting
wykrój	**6.** pattern piece	wełna	**23.** wool
zestaw wykrojów	**7.** pattern	motek	**24.** skein
dziurka do guzika	**8.** buttonhole	drut	**25.** knitting needle
guzik	**9.** button	koronka robiona igłą	**26.** needlepoint
szew	**10.** seam	haft	**27.** embroidery
rąbek	**11.** hem	robota szydełkowa	**28.** crochet
lamówka	**12.** hem binding	szydełko	**29.** crochet hook
zatrzask	**13.** snap	tkanie	**30.** weaving
haftka	**14.** hook and eye	przędza	**31.** yarn
metr krawiecki	**15.** tape measure	pikowanie, watowanie	**32.** quilting
zamek błyskawiczny	**16.** zipper		
nożyczki	**17.** (pair of) scissors		
igła	**18.** needle		

przy (oknie)	**1.** at (the window)
ponad (czarnym kotem)	**2.** above (the black cat)
poniżej (białego kota)	**3.** below (the white cat)
pomiędzy (poduszkami)	**4.** between (the pillows)
na (dywanie)	**5.** on (the rug)

na wprost (kominka)	**6.** in front of (the fireplace)
w (szufladzie)	**7.** in (the drawer)
pod (biurkiem)	**8.** under (the desk)
za (krzesłem)	**9.** behind (the chair)
na wierzchu (stołu)	**10.** on top of (the table)
obok (telewizora)	**11.** next to (the TV)

poprzez (latarnię morską)	**1.** through (the lighthouse)
obok (latarni morskiej)	**2.** around (the lighthouse)
w dół (wzgórza)	**3.** down (the hill)
ku (dołkowi)	**4.** toward (the hole)
od (dołka)	**5.** away from (the hole)
ponad, poprzez (wodę)	**6.** across (the water)

z (wody)	**7.** out of (the water)
przez (most)	**8.** over (the bridge)
na (tor)	**9.** to (the course)
z (toru)	**10.** from (the course)
pod (górę)	**11.** up (the hill)
do (dołka)	**12.** into (the hole)

Dni tygodnia	**Days of the Week**
niedziela	Sunday
poniedziałek	Monday
wtorek	Tuesday
środa	Wednesday
czwartek	Thursday
piątek	Friday
sobota	Saturday

Miesiące	**Months of the Year**
styczeń	January
luty	February
marzec	March
kwiecień	April
maj	May
czerwiec	June
lipiec	July
sierpień	August
wrzesień	September
październik	October
listopad	November
grudzień	December

Liczby		**Numbers**
zero	0	zero
jeden	1	one
dwa	2	two
trzy	3	three
cztery	4	four
pięć	5	five
sześć	6	six
siedem	7	seven
osiem	8	eight
dziewięć	9	nine
dziesięć	10	ten
jedenaście	11	eleven
dwanaście	12	twelve
trzynaście	13	thirteen
czternaście	14	fourteen
piętnaście	15	fifteen
szesnaście	16	sixteen
siedemnaście	17	seventeen
osiemnaście	18	eighteen
dziewiętnaście	19	nineteen
dwadzieścia	20	twenty
dwadzieścia jeden	21	twenty-one
trzydzieści	30	thirty
czterdzieści	40	forty
pięćdziesiąt	50	fifty
sześćdziesiąt	60	sixty
siedemdziesiąt	70	seventy
osiemdziesiąt	80	eighty
dziewięćdziesiąt	90	ninety
sto	100	a/one hundred
pięćset	500	five hundred
sześćset dwadzieścia jeden	621	six hundred (and) twenty-one
tysiąc	1,000	a/one thousand
milion	1,000,000	a/one million

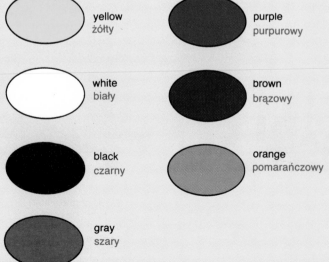

Kolory **Colors**

red czerwony	green zielony
blue niebieski	pink różowy
yellow żółty	purple purpurowy
white biały	brown brązowy
black czarny	orange pomarańczowy
gray szary	

Two numbers occur after words in the index: the first refers to the page where the word is illustrated and the second to the item number of the word on that page. For example, above [ə bŭv⁄] **102** 2 means that the word *above* is the item numbered 2 on page 102. If only a bold number appears, then that word is part of the unit title or a subtitle.

The index includes a pronunciation guide for all the words illustrated in the book. This guide uses symbols commonly found in dictionaries for native speakers. These symbols, unlike those used in transcription systems such as the International Phonetic Alphabet, tend to preserve spelling and so should help you to become more aware of the connections between written English and spoken English.

Consonants

[b] as in **back** [băk]   [k] as in **kite** [kīt]   [sh] as in **shell** [shĕl]
[ch] as in **cheek** [chēk]   [l] as in **leaf** [lēf]   [t] as in **tape** [tāp]
[d] as in **date** [dāt]   [m] as in **man** [măn]   [th] as in **three** [thrē]
[dh] as in **the** [dh]   [n] as in **neck** [nĕk]   [v] as in **vine** [vīn]
[f] as in **face** [fās]   [ng] as·in **ring** [rĭng]   [w] as in **waist** [wāst]
[g] as in **gas** [găs]   [p] as in **pack** [păk]   [y] as in **yam** [yăm]
[h] as in **half** [hăf]   [r] as in **rake** [rāk]   [z] as in **zoo** [zo͞o]
[j] as in **jack** [jăk]   [s] as in **sand** [sănd]   [zh] as in **measure** [mĕzh⁄ər]

Vowels

[ā] as in **bake** [bāk]   [ī] as in **lime** [līm]   [o͞o] as in **cool** [ko͞ol]
[ă] as in **back** [băk]   [ĭ] as in **lip** [lĭp]   [o͝o] as in **book** [bo͝ok]
[ä] as in **bar** [bär]   [ï] as in **beer** [bïr]   [ow] as in **cow** [kow]
[ē] as in **beat** [bēt]   [ō] as in **post** [pōst]   [oy] as in **boy** [boy]
[ĕ] as in **bed** [bĕd]   [ŏ] as in **box** [bŏks]   [ŭ] as in **cut** [kŭt]
[ë] as in **bear** [bër]   [ö] as in **claw** [klö]   [ü] as in **curb** [kürb]
                                       or **for** [för]   [ə] as in **above** [ə bŭv⁄]

All pronunciation symbols used are alphabetical except for the schwa [ə], which is the most frequent vowel sound in English. If you use it appropriately in unstressed syllables, your pronunciation will sound more natural.

You should note that an umlaut ([¨]) calls attention to the special quality of vowels before [r]. (The sound [ö] can also represent a vowel not followed by [r] as in *claw.*) You should listen carefully to native speakers to discover how these vowels actually sound.

Stress

This guide also follows the system for marking stress used in many dictionaries for native speakers.
  (1) Stress is not marked if a word consisting of a single syllable occurs in isolation.
  (2) Where stress is marked, two levels are distinguished:
    a bold accent [**/**] is placed after each syllable with primary stress,
    a light accent [/] is placed after each syllable with secondary stress.

Syllable Boundaries

Syllable boundaries are indicated by a single space.

NOTE: The pronunciation used in this index is based on patterns of American English. There has been no attempt to represent all of the varieties of American English. Students should listen to native speakers to hear how the language actually sounds in a particular region.

above [ə bŭv/] **102** 2

abdomen [ăb/də mən] **4** 14

accelerator [ăk sĕl/ə rā/tər] **50** 27

accordion [ə kör/dē ən] **98** 28

accountant [ə kown/tənt] **86** 18

acorn [ā/körn] **61** 33b

acorn squash [ā/körn skwŏsh/] **7** 28

across [ə krös/] **103** 6

actor [ăk/tər] **99** 19

actress [ăk/trəs] **99** 20

acute angle [ə kyōōt/ ăng/gəl] **79** 8

address [ă/drĕs] **46** 11

adjectives [ăj/ĭk tĭvz] **24, 25**

aerial tramway [ër/ē əl trăm/wā] **55** 31

Africa [ă/frĭ kə] **70** 4

after-shave lotion [ăf/tər shāv lō/shən] **23** 21

ailments [āl/mənts] **40**

air conditioner [ër/kən dĭ/shə nər] **32** 11

air filter [ër/fĭl/tər] **51** 52

Air Force [ër/förs/] **48** 19

air mattress [ër/mă/trəs] **91** 26

air pump [ër/ pŭmp/] **53** 13

air travel [ër/ tră/vəl] **56**

aircraft [ër/krăft/] **57**

aircraft carrier [ër/krăft kăr/yər] **48** 4

aircraft types [ër/krăft tīps/] **57**

(airmail) envelope [ër/māl ĕn/və lōp] **46** 16

airman [ër/mən] **48** 20

airport check-in [ër/pört chĕk/ĭn] **56**

aisle [ī/əl] **14** 10, **56** 23

Alabama [ăl/ə bă/mə] **72** 1

alarm clock [ə lärm/ klŏk] **32** 8

Alaska [ə lăs/kə] **72** 2

alcohol [ăl/kə höl/] **39** 22

alligator [ăl/ə gā/tər] **65** 8

almond(s) [ö/mənd(z)] **9** 31

Alps [ălps] **70** 44

Amazon River [ă/mə zŏn rĭv/ər] **71** 59

ambulance [ăm/byə ləns] **42** 6

amphibians [ăm fĭ/bē ənz] **65**

ammunition [ăm/yə nĭsh/ən] **48**

anchor [ăng/kər] **58** 24

Andes [ăn/dēz] **71** 43

ankle [ăng/kəl] **5** 49

animals [ăn/ə məlz] **62-69**

ant [ănt] **63** 12

Antarctic Ocean [ănt ärk/tĭk ō/ shən] **70** 14

Antarctica [ănt ärk/tĭ kə] **70** 7

anteater [ănt/ē/tər] **66** 5

antenna [ăn tĕn/ə] **51** 46, **62** 1b

antler [ănt/lər] **67** 35a

apartment house [ə pärt/mənt hows/] **45** 23

apex [ā/pĕks] **79** 21

Appalachian Mountains [ăp/ə lā/chē ən mown/ tənz] **71** 41

apple [ă/pəl] **8** 2

apricot [ăp/rə kŏt/] **9** 25

apron [ā/prən] **16** 6

aquatic mammals [ə kwŏ/tĭk·mă/məlz] **68**

Arabian Sea [ə rā/bē ən sē/] **70** 30

arc [ärk] **79** 16

architect [är/kə tĕkt/] **86** 8

Arctic [ärk/tĭk] **70** 8

Arizona [ăr/ə zō/nə] **72** 3

Arkansas [är/kən sö/] **72** 4

arm [ärm] **4** 6, **100** 20

armadillo [är/mə dĭl/ō] **66** 2

armed forces [ärmd/ för/səz] **48**

armpit [ärm/pĭt/] **4** 10

armrest [ärm/rĕst/] **50** 3

Army [är/mē] **48** 15

around [ə rownd/] **103** 2

artery [är/tə rē] **5** 69

artichoke [är/tə chōk/] **6** 11

artist [är/təst] **86** 3

arts [ärts] **86**

ashtray [ăsh/trā/] **16** 29

Asia [ā/zhə] **70** 5

asparagus [ə spăr/ə gəs] **6** 18

asteroid [ăs/tə royd/] **74** 20

astronaut [ăs/trə nöt/] **75** 5

at [ăt] **102** 1

Atacama Desert [ăt/ə kŏ/mə dĕz/ərt] **71** 50

athletic supporter [ăth lĕ/tĭk sə pör/tər] **22** 4

atlas [ăt/ləs] **47** 20

attachments [ə tăch/mənts] **35** 17

attendant [ə tĕn/dənt] **39** 8, **53** 12

audience [ö/dē əns] **99** 15

audio [ö/dē ō/] **100**

aunt [ănt] **3** 6

Australia [ö strāl/yə] **70** 6

author [ö/thər] **47** 8

automatic transmission [ö/ tə măt/ĭk trănz mĭ/shən] **50**

avocado [ăv/ə kŏ/dō] **9** 33

away from [ə wā/ frŭm] **103** 5

axe [ăks] **42** 14

baboon [bă bōōn/] **69** 19

baby [bā/bē] **2** 5

baby carriage [bā/bē kăr/ĭj] **45** 27

baby lotion [bā/bē lō/shən] **33** 6

baby powder [bā/bē pow/dər] **33** 7

baby wipes [bā/bē wīps/] **33** 8

baby's room [bā/bēz rōōm/] **33**

back [băk] **4** 11, **23** 19

backache [băk/āk/] **40** 8

backboard [băk/börd/] **92** 19

backhoe [băk/hō/] **82** 26

backpack [băk/păk/] **19** 4

backseat [băk/sēt/] **50** 32

backyard [băk/yärd/] **27**

back-up light [băk/əp līt/] **50** 30

bacon [bā/kən] **10** 11, **18**, 33

badge [băj] **43** 5

Baffin Bay [băf/ən bā/] **70** 16

bag [băg] **12** 8, **15** 25, **21** 35

baggage [băg/ĭj] **56** 8

bake [bāk] **31** 14

baked beans [bākt/ bēnz/] **18** 3

baked goods [bākt gŏŏdz/] **14** 11

baked potato [bākt/ pə tā/tō] **18** 20

baker [bā/kər] **84** 8

bakery [bā/kə rē] **44** 6

balance beam [băl/əns bēm/] **94** 24

balcony [băl/kə nē] **99** 14

(bale of) hay [bāl/ əv hā/] **81** 13

ball [böl] **5** 52

ballet [bă lā/] **99**

ballfields [böl/fēldz/] **93**

ballpoint pen [böl/poynt pĕn/] **76** 22

Baltic Sea [böl/tĭk sē/] **70** 22

bananas [bə nă/nəz] **9** 20

Band-Aid [bănd/ ād/] **39** 4

band shell [bănd/ shĕl/] **87** 2

bandage [băn/dĭj] **39** 24

banister [băn′ə stər] **28** 11

banjo [băn′jō′] **98** 5

banking [băng′kĭng] **86**

bar [bär] **13** 18, **16** 24

bar stool [bär′stool′] **16** 25

barber [bär′bər] **84** 3

Barents Sea [băr′ənts sē′] **70** 23

barge [bärj] **58** 12

bark [bärk] **61** 35c

barn [bärn] **81** 5

barnyard [bärn′yärd′] **81** 8

barrel [băr′əl] **48** 23

barricade [băr′ə kād′] **82** 21

bartender [bär′těn′dər] **16** 21

base [bās] **79** 7, **93** 6

baseball [bās′böl′] **92**

baseball diamond [bās′böl dī′mənd]
   93

baseline [bās′līn′] **95** 4

basin [bā′sən] **39** 16

basket [băs′kət] **92** 20

basketball [băs′kət böl′] **92**, **92** 21

bass [bās] **98** 10

bass guitarist [bās′gə tär′əst] **99** 23

bassoon [bă soon′] **98** 14

bat [băt] **66** 4, **92** 5

batboy [băt′boy′] **93** 18

bath mat [băth′ măt′] **34** 12

bath towel [băth′ tow′əl] **34** 24

bathing suit [bā′dhĭng soot′] **90** 18

bathing trunks [bā′ dhĭng trŭngks′]
   91 33

bathrobe [băth′ rōb′] **22** 20

bathroom [băth′ room′] **34**

bathtub [băth′ tŭb′] **34** 11

baton [bə tŏn′] **99** 9

batter [băt′ ər] **92** 7, **93** 14

battery [băt′ə rē] **51** 54

batting helmet [băt′ĭng hĕl′mət] **92** 6

battleship [băt′əl shĭp′] **48** 5

Bay of Bengal [bā′ əv běn göl′] **70** 32

bayonet [bā′ə nět′] **48** 24

bays [bāz] **70**

beach [bēch] **90**

beach ball [bēch′ böl′] **90** 11

beach chair [bēch′ chěr′] **90** 20

beach towel [bēch′ tow′ əl] **90** 15

beach umbrella [bēch′əm brěl′ə]
   90 21

beads [bēdz] **23** 7

beak [bēk] **64** 3a

beaker [bē′kər] **78** 23

beard [bïrd] **4** 39

bears [běrz] **69**

beat [bēt] **31** 8

Beaufort Sea [bō′ fərt sē′] **70** 15

beaver [bē′vər] **66** 12

bed [běd] **32** 21

bed rest [běd′ rěst′] **41** 1

bedroom [běd′room′] **32**

bedspread [běd′sprěd′] **32** 23

bee [bē] **63** 19

beef [bēf] **10** 1

beef stew [bēf′ stoo′] **18** 14

beer [bïr] **16** 23

beet(s) [bēts] **7** 33

beetle [bē′təl] **63** 10

behind [bə hīnd′] **102** 9

below [bə lō′] **102** 3

belt [bělt] **20** 16

bench [běnch] **43** 16, **44** 14, **78** 24,
   87 10

beret [bə rā′] **19** 22

Bering Sea [běr′ĭng sē′] **70** 34

berries [běr′ēz] **8**

between [bə twēn′] **102** 4

beverages [běv′rə jəz] **14** 14

bib [bĭb] **33** 20

bicycle [bī′sĭ kəl] **52** 15

big [bĭg] **24** 8

(Big Dipper) constellation
   [bĭg′dĭ′pər kŏn stə lā′shən] **74** 3

big toe [bĭg′ tō′] **5** 53

bike stand [bīk′ stănd′] **52** 14

biker [bī′kər] **90** 4

bikes [bīks] **52**

(bikini) panties [bə kē′ nē păn′ tēz]
   22 11

bill [bĭl] **64** 24a

bin [bĭn] **15** 16

binding [bīn′ dĭng] **95** 16

binoculars [bə nŏk′ yə lərs] **90** 7

birch [bürch] **61** 32

birds [bürdz] **64**

biscuit [bĭs′ kət] **18** 27

bison [bī′sən] **67** 19

bit [bĭt] **37** 43a

black bear [blăk′ běr′] **69** 21

black bean(s) [blăk′ bēn(z)′] **6** 14

black eye [blăk′ ī′] **40** 5

Black Sea [blăk′ sē′] **70** 26

blackberries [blăk′ běr′ ēz] **8** 12

bladder [blă′ dər] **5** 72

blade [blād] **94** 27

blanket [blăng′ket] **32** 20

blazer [blā′zer] **20** 2

bleach [blēch] **35** 26

blender [blěn′dər] **30** 12

blimp [blĭmp] **57** 5

blinds [blīndz] **32** 12

block [blŏk] **33** 32

blouse [blows] **21** 34

blue jay [bloo′ ja′] **64** 8

(blue) jeans [bloo′ jēnz′] **19** 6

blueberries [bloo′běr′ēz] **8** 14

blueprints [bloo′prĭnts′] **82** 6

blush [blŭsh] **23** 32

board [börd] **82** 16

boarding [bör′dĭng] **56**

boarding pass [bör′dĭng păs′] **56** 18

boardwalk [börd′wök′] **90** 1

body [bŏ′dē] **4**

boil [boyl] **31** 16

bollard [bŏl′ərd] **58** 26

bolt [bōlt] **37** 38

bomb [bŏm] **48** 3

bomber [bŏm′ ər] **48** 2

bongos [bŏng′ gōz] **98** 22

book [book] **13** 17

(book of) matches [book′ əv mă′ chəz]
   16 28

bookcase [book′ kās] **28** 22, **83** 20

bookstore [book′ stör] **45** 18

boom [boom] **59** 7

booth [booth] **16** 9

boots [boots] **19** 21, **21** 32

bottle [bŏt′ əl] **12** 3, **33** 17

bottle opener [bŏt′ əl ō′ pə nər] **30** 6

bounce [bowns] **97** 11

bow [bō] **98** 7a

bow [bow] **58** 5

bowl [bōl] **13** 23

bowling [bōl′ĭng] **94**

bowling ball [bōl′ĭng bôl′] **94** 6

box [bŏks] **13** 12

box seat [bŏks′ sēt′] **99** 11

box spring [bŏks′ sprĭng′] **32** 18

boxer shorts [bŏk′ sər shörts′] **22** 2

boxing [bŏk′ sĭng] **94**

boy's frame [boyz′ frām′] **52** 11

bra(ssiere) [brŏ]/[brə zïr′] **22** 13

brace [brās] **36** 9

bracelet [brās′lət] **23** 9

brain [brān] **5** 57

brake [brāk] **50** 26, **52** 17

brake light [brāk′ līt′] **50** 29

branch [brănch] **61** 35a

brass [brăs] **98**

bread [brĕd] **14** 12

bread and butter plate
  [brĕd′ ənd bŭt′ ər plāt′] **29** 11

break [brāk] **31** 7

breast [brĕst] **11** 21

bricks [brĭks] **82** 12

bridle path [brīd′ əl păth′] **87** 7

briefcase [brēf′kās′] **21** 37

briefs [brēfs] **22** 12

broccoli [brŏk′ ə lē] **6** 2

broil [broyl] **31** 13

broiler [broy′lər] **30** 33

broken bone [brō′kən bōn′] **40** 15

broom [broom] **35** 7

brother [brŭdh′ ər] **3** 9

brother-in-law [brŭdh′ ər ən lö′] **3** 11

bruise [brooz] **40** 17

brush [brŭsh] **76** 18

brussels sprouts [brŭs′ əl sprowts′] **6** 4

bucket [bŭk′ət] **35** 15

bucket seat [bŭk′ət sēt′] **50** 16

buckle [bŭk′ əl] **20** 17

bud [bŭd] **60** 18a

buffet [bə fā′] **29** 29

builder [bĭl′dər] **82** 5

building number [bĭl′ dĭng nŭm′ bər]
  45 24

bulb [bŭlb] **60** 8a

bull [bool] **67** 34

bulldozer [bool′dō′ zər] **82** 27

bullet [bool′ĭt] **48** 26

bulletin board [bool′ ĭ tən börd′] **76** 7

bumper [bŭm′pər] **33** 5

bun [bŭn] **18** 7

bunch [bŭnch] **8** 1

Bunsen burner [bŭn′sən bür′ nər]
  78 20

buoy [boo′ē]/[boy] **58** 16

bureau [byoor′ō] **32** 9

burn [bürn] **17** 14, **40** 18

burner [bür′nər] **30** 29

bus [bŭs] **53** 20, **54**

bus driver [bŭs′drī′vər] **54** 3

bus stop [bŭs′stŏp′] **44** 13

busboy [bŭs′boy′] **16** 3

bushes [boosh′ əz] **61** 41

business workers [biz′nəs wür′kərz] **86**

butcher [boo′chər] **84** 13

butter [bŭt′ər] **18** 18

buttercup [bŭt′ ər kŭp′] **60** 17

butterfly [bŭt′ ər flī′] **63** 3

buttocks [bŭt′əks] **4** 15

button [bŭt′ən] **20** 3, **101** 9

buttonhole [bŭt′ ən hōl′] **101** 8

C-clamp [sē′klămp′] **36** 2

cab driver [kăb′drī′ vər] **55** 26

cabbage [kăb′ĭj] **6** 3

cabin [kăb′ĭn] **56** 19

cabin cruiser [kăb′ĭn kroo′ zər] **59** 16

cabinet [kăb′ə nət] **30** 22

cable [kā′bəl] **52** 23

cable car [kā′bəl kär′] **55** 32

cactus [kăk′təs] **61** 40

calculator [kăl′kyə lā′ tər] **83** 19,
  100 34

calendar [căl′ ən dər] **83** 9

calf [kăf] **4** 20, **67** 31

California [kăl′ ə för′ nyə] **72** 5

call card [köl′kärd′] **47** 6

call number [köl′nŭm′ bər] **47** 6

call slip [köl′slĭp′] **47** 12

camel [kăm′ əl] **67** 33

camera [kăm′ər ə] **100** 8

cameraperson [kăm′ ər ə pür′ sən] **86** 10

camisole [kăm′ ə sōl′] **22** 9

camp stove [kămp′ stōv′] **89** 25

camper [kăm′pər] **53** 16

campfire [kămp′fīr′] **89** 31

camping [kăm′pĭng] **89**

can [kăn] **12** 10

can opener [kăn′ ō′ pə nər] **30** 4

canary [kə nër′ ē] **64** 14

candle [kăn′dəl] **29** 27

candlestick [kăn′dəl stĭk′] **29** 28

canister [kăn′ə stər] **30** 15

canned goods [kănd′ goodz′] **14** 13

cannon [kăn′ ən] **48** 11

canoe [kə noo′] **59** 2

cantaloupe [kăn′ tə lōp′] **9** 36

canyon [kăn′ yən] **88** 3

cap [kăp] **19** 2, **21** 43, **92** 11

capsule [kăp′ səl] **41** 5

car [kär] **54** 9

card catalog [kärd′ kăt′ ə lög] **47** 4

cardigan [kär′dĭ gən] **21** 26

cardinal [kärd′nəl] **64** 11

cargo [kär′gō] **58** 10

cargo area [kär′gō ër′ ē ə] **57** 12

cargo bay [kär′gō bā′] **75** 9

cargo door [kär′gō dör′] **57** 13

Caribbean Sea [kăr′ ə bē′ ən sē′]
  70 20

carpenter [kär′pən tər] **85** 2

carpenter's rule [kär′ pən tərz rool′]
  36 1

carrot(s) [kăr′ ət(s)] **7** 32

carry [kăr′ē] **26** 16

carry-on bag [kăr′ē ŏn băg′] **56** 2

cars [kärz] **50-51**

carton [kär′tən] **12** 1

cartridge needle [kär′trĭj nē′ dəl]
  100 19

carve [kärv] **31** 6

cash register [kăsh′rĕ′ jə stər] **15** 21

cashew(s) [kăsh′ oo(z)] **9** 27

cashier [kă shïr′] **15** 22

Caspian Sea [kăs′pē ən sē′] **70** 27

casserole dish [kăs′ ə rōl dĭsh′] **30** 14

cassette [kə sĕt′] **100** 26

cassette deck [kə sĕt′ dĕk′] **100** 22

cast [kăst] **39** 5

cat [kăt] **68** 4

catch [kăch] **96** 4

catcher [kăch′ ər] **92** 2, **93** 16

catcher's mask [kăch′ərz măsk′] **92** 3

catcher's mitt [kăch′ərz mĭt′] **92** 4

caterpillar [kăt′ər pĭl′ər] **63** 1

cattle [kăt′ əl] **81** 20

Caucasus [kö′kə səs] **71** 45

cauliflower [kŏl′ ə flow′ ər] **6** 1
ceiling [sē′lĭng] **28** 2
ceiling fan [sē ′lĭng făn′] **28** 1
celery [sĕl′ ə rē] **6** 10
cello [chĕl′o] **98** 9
cement [sə mĕnt′] **82** 10
cement mixer [sə mĕnt′ mĭk′ sər]
　82 25
cement truck [sə mĕnt′ trŭk′] **49** 13
center [sĕn′tər] **79** 13, **93** 27
center divider [sĕn′ tər də vī′ dər]
　53 18, **82** 24
center fielder [sĕn′ tər fēl′ dər] **93** 2
center lane [sĕn′ tər lān′] **53** 6
centerboard [sĕn′ tər börd′] **59** 6
centipede [sĕn′ tə pēd′] **63** 22
chain [chān] **23** 5, **52** 18
chair [chër] **29** 17
chalk [chök] **76** 10
chalk tray [chök′ trā′] **76** 9
chalkboard [chök′ börd′] **76** 5
chandelier [shăn′ də lïr′] **29** 3
change (the sheets) [chānj′ dhə shēts′]
　38 13
changing table [chān′ jĭng tā′ bəl] **33** 9
charcoal briquettes
　[chär′ kōl brĭ kĕts′] **27** 23
chart [chärt] **39** 10
check [chĕk] **15** 27, **16** 14
checked [chĕkt] **24** 18
checkout counter [chĕk′ owt kown′ tər]
　15 26
checkout desk [chĕk′ owt dĕsk′] **47** 2
cheerleaders [chïr′ lē′ dərz] **93** 20
cheek [chēk] **4** 35
cherries [chër′ ēz] **9** 19
cherry picker [chër′ ē pĭk′ ər] **82** 18
chest [chĕst] **4** 12
chest of drawers [chĕst′ əv drörz′]
　32 30
chestnut(s) [chĕs′ nŭt(s)] **9** 32
chick [chĭk] **64** 22
chicken [chĭk′ ən] **11** 24, **64** 23
child's seat [chīldz′ sēt′] **50** 33
children [chĭl′ drən] **2** 7
chills [chĭlz] **40** 4
chimney [chĭm′ nē] **27** 9
chimpanzee [chĭm păn′ zē] **69** 16

chin [chĭn] **4** 3
china [chī′ nə] **29** 1
china closet [chī′ nə klōz′ ət] **29** 2
chipmunk [chĭp′ mŭnk] **66** 6
chop [chŏp] **26** 11, **31** 11
chops [chŏps] **10** 9, **10** 15
chorus [kör′ əs] **99** 18
(chrysanthe)mum
　[krə săn′ thə məm]/[mŭm] **60** 4
cigarette [sĭg′ ə rĕt′] **16** 31
circle [sür′ kəl] **79** 11
circuit breaker [sür′ kət brā′ kər] **35** 5
circular saw [sür′ kyə lər sö′] **36** 20
circumference [sür kŭm′ fə rəns] **79** 17
citrus fruits [sĭ′ trəs frōōts′] **8**
city [sĭt′ ē] **44-45**
clam(s) [klăm(z)] **11** 32
clamp [klămp] **78** 7
clarinet [klăr′ ə nĕt′] **98** 16
clasp [klăsp] **23** 17
classroom [klăs′ rōōm′] **76**
claw [klö] **62** 13a, **68** 2a
clean [klēn] **24** 6, **26** 2
cleanser [klĕn′ zər] **35** 9
clear [klïr] **17** 6
cliff [klĭf] **89** 21
clip-on earring [klĭp′ ŏn ïr′ ĭng] **23** 15
clock [klŏk] **76** 2
close (v) [klōz] **77** 5
closed [klōzd] **24** 16
closet [klŏz′ ət] **32** 3
cloth diaper [klöth′ dī′ pər] **33** 13
clothes [klōz] **19-24**
clothesline [klōz′ līn′] **35** 19
clothespins [klōz′ pĭnz′] **35** 20
cloudy [klow′ dē] **25** 2
clove [klōv] **7** 25a
cloverleaf [klō′ vər lēf′] **53** 4
clubs [klŭbz] **95** 5
clutch [klŭch] **50** 25
coach [kōch] **93** 21
coal [kōl] **80** 7
coal mine [kōl′ mīn′] **80** 6
coaster [kō′ stər] **16** 27
coat [kōt] **19** 24, **42** 13
cob [kŏb] **6** 12a
cobra [kō′ brə] **65** 11
cockpit [kŏk′ pĭt′] **56** 13

cockroach [kŏk′ rōch′] **63** 9
cocktail lounge [kŏk′ tāl lownj′] **16**
cocktail waitress [kŏk′ tāl wā′ trəs]
　16 32
cocoon [kə kōōn′] **63** 2
coconut [kō′ kə nŭt′] **8** 3
coffee [kö′ fē] **18** 35
coffeemaker [kö′ fē mā′ kər] **30** 31
coffeepot [kö′ fē pŏt′] **29** 18
coffee table [kö′ fē tā′ bəl] **28** 26
coins [koynz] **13** 26
colander [kŏl′ ən dər] **30** 7
cold [kōld] **25** 10, **40** 11
cold water faucet [kōld′ wŏ tər fö′ sət]
　34 18
collar [kŏl′ ər] **20** 20
colonial-style house
　[kə lō′ nē əl stīl hows′] **27**
Colorado [kŏl′ ə rŏd′ ō] **72** 6
column [kŏl′ əm] **50** 13
comb [kōm] **32** 6
combine (n) [kŏm′ bīn] **81** 17
comet [kŏm′ ət] **74** 2
comforter [kŭm′ fər tər] **32** 22
command module [kə mănd′ mŏj′ ōōl]
　75 8
communication satellite
　[kə myōō′ nə kā shən săt′ ə līt] **75** 2
commuter [kə myōō′ tər] **55** 17
commuter train [kə myōō′ tər trān′]
　55 14
compact disc (CD)
　[kŏm′ păkt dĭsk′]/[sē′ dē′] **100** 27
compact disc player
　[kŏm′ păkt dĭsk′ plā′ ər] **100** 28
computer [kəm pyōō′ tər] **76** 8, **83**
　16, **100**
computer programmer
　[kəm pyōō′ tər prō′ grăm ər] **86** 16
conductor [kən dŭk′ tər] **54** 7, **99** 8
cone [kōn] **61** 34b, **79** 28, **82** 19
conga [kŏng′ gə] **98** 20
Congo River [kŏng′ gō rĭv′ ər] **71** 62
Connecticut [kə nĕ′ tĭ kət] **72** 7
constellation [kŏn′ stə lā′ shən] **74** 3
construction [kən strŭk′ shən] **82**
(construction) boots
　[kən strŭk′ shən bōōts′] **21** 32

construction site [kən strŭk′ shən sīt′] **82**

construction worker
  [kən strŭk′ shən wür′ kər] **82** 14

container [kən tā′nər] **12** 2, **58** 7

(container)ship [kən tā′ nər shĭp′] **58** 9

containers [kən tā′ nərz] **12**

continents [kŏn′ tə nənts] **70**

control tower [kən trōl′ tow′ər] **57** 20

conveyor belt [kən vā′ər bĕlt] **15** 23,
  56 12

cook (n) [kŏŏk] **17** 4

cook (v) [kŏŏk] **17** 4

cookie [kŏŏk′ ē] **18** 22

cool [kōŏl] **25** 9

cooler [kōŏ′ lər] **91** 41

cooling tower [kōŏ′lĭng tow′ər] **80** 16

copilot [kō′pī lət] **56** 16

cord [körd] **32** 26a, **54** 1

(corduroy) pants [kör′ də roy pănts′]
  21 27

core [kör] **8** 2b, **80** 14

cork [körk] **16** 18

corkscrew [körk′ skrōŏ′] **16** 17

corn [körn] **6** 12, **60** 24

corner [kör′ nər] **44** 3

corral [kə răl′] **81** 24

cosmetics [kŏz mĕt′ ĭks] **23**

cotton balls [kŏt′ ən bölz′] **39** 23

cotton swab [kŏt′ ən swŏb′] **33** 10

counter [kown′ tər] **30** 27

court [kört] **43**, **94** 13

court officer [kört′ ö′ fə sər] **43** 19

court reporter [kört′ rə pör′ tər] **43** 14

cousin [kŭz′ən] **3** 7

cow [kow] **67** 32

cowboy [kow′ boy′] **81** 21

cowgirl [kow′ gürl′] **81** 22

crab(s) [krǎ b(z)] **11** 36, **62** 9

cradle [krā′ dəl] **33** 26

cranberries [krăn′ bër′ ēz] **8** 13

crane [krān] **58** 6

creamer [krē′ mər] **29** 24

crew [krōŏ] **75** 12

(crewneck) sweater
  [krōŏ′ nĕk swĕt′ ər] **19** 7

crib [krĭb] **33** 4

criket [krĭk′ ət] **63** 5

crime [krīm] **43**

crochet [krō shā′] **101** 28

crochet hook [krō′ shā′ hŏŏk′] **101** 29

crocus [krō′ kəs] **60** 9

cross-country skiing
  [krös′ kŭn trē skē′ ĭng] **94**

crosswalk [krös′ wök′] **44** 4

crow [krō] **64** 3

crutch [krŭch] **39** 7

cube [kyōŏb] **79** 27

cubicle [kyōŏ′ bə kəl] **83** 5

cucumber(s) [kyōŏ′ kŭm bər(z)] **7** 20

cuff links [kŭf′ lĭnks′] **23** 12

cup [kŭp] **13** 19, **29** 20

curb [kürb] **45** 26

curtain [kür′ tən] **32** 10, **99** 1

curtain rings [kür′ tən rĭngz′] **34** 2

curtain rod [kür′ tən rŏd′] **34** 1

curve [kürv] **79** 3

cushion [kŏŏsh′ ən] **28** 24

customer [kŭs′ tə mər] **15** 17

cut (v) [kŭt] **31** 9

cut (n) [kŭt] **40** 16

cutting board [kŭt′ ĭng börd′] **30** 26

cylinder [sĭl′ ĭn dər] **79** 26

cymbals [sĭm′ bəlz] **98** 18

daffodil [dăf′ ə dĭl] **60** 8

dairy cow [dër′ ē kow′] **81** 11

dairy farm [dër′ ē färm′] **81**

dairy products [dër′ ē prŏd′ ŭkts] **14** 4

daisy [dā′ zē] **60** 5

dam [dăm] **80** 18

dance [dăns] **99**

dancer [dăn′ sər] **99** 3

dark [därk] **24** 10

dashboard [dăsh′ börd′] **50** 19

date [dāt] **9** 23

daughter [dö′ tər] **3** 15

deck [dĕk] **27** 5, **58** 22

deer [dĭr] **67** 26

defendant [də fĕn′ dənt] **43** 23

defense attorney [də fĕns′ ə tür′ nē]
  43 22

Delaware [dĕl′ ə wăr′] **72** 8

deli counter [dĕl′ ē kown′ tər] **14** 1

delivery boy [də lĭv′ ə rē boy′] **85** 10

delivery person [də lĭv′ ə rē pür′ sən]
  49 10

dental care [dĕn′ təl kër′] **39**

dentist [dĕn′ tĭst] **39** 17

department store [də pärt′ mənt stör′]
  44 5

depth [dĕpth] **79** 33

derrick [dĕr′ ĭk] **80** 2

deserts [dĕz′ ərts] **71**

desk [dĕsk] **28** 14, **76** 16, **83** 13

detective [də tĕk′ tĭv] **43** 2

diagonal [dī ăg′ ə nəl] **79** 20

diameter [dī ăm′ ə tər] **79** 12

dictionary [dĭk′ shə nër′ ē] **47** 24

diesel fuel [dē′ zəl fyōŏ′ əl] **80** 34

dig [dĭg] **26** 3

dime [dīm] **13** 29

dinghy [dĭng′ ē] **59** 18

dining room [dī′ nĭng rōŏm′] **29**

dipstick [dĭp′ stĭk′] **51** 58

dirt bike [dürt′ bīk′] **52** 8

disc jockey (DJ) [dĭsk′ jŏk′ ē]/[dē′ jā]
  86 9

dirty [dür′ tē] **24** 5

dish drainer [dĭsh′ drā′ nər] **30** 2

dish towel [dĭsh′ tow′ əl] **30** 18

dishwasher [dĭsh′ wŏsh′ ər] **30** 1

dishwashing liquid
  [dĭsh′ wŏsh ĭng lĭ′ kwĭd] **30** 10

disposable diaper
  [dĭs pō′ zə bəl dī′ pər] **33** 12

dissection kit [dĭ sĕk′ shən kĭt′] **78** 33

dive [dīv] **97** 14

dock [dŏk] **58** 28

doctor [dŏk′ tər] **39** 11

dogs [dögz] **69**

dogwood [dög′ wŏŏd′] **61** 28

doll [dŏl] **33** 28

doll house [dŏl′ hows′] **33** 25

dollar bills [dŏl′ər bĭlz′] **13** 25

dolly [dŏl′ ē] **56** 6

dolphin [dŏl′ fĭn] **68** 13

donkey [dŏng′ kē] **67** 23

door handle [dör′ hăn′ dəl] **50** 4

door lock [dör′ lŏk′] **50** 1

doorman [dör′ mən] **85** 11

down [down] **103** 3

down vest [down′ vĕst′] **19** 12

dragonfly [drăg′ ən flī′] **63** 4

drain [drān] **34** 9

drainpipe [drān′ pīp′] **27** 18

drapes [drāps] **28** 23

draw [drö] **77** 11

drawer [drör] **47** 5

dress [drĕs] **20** 22

dried fruits [drīd/ frōōts/] **9**

drill [drĭl] **39** 15

drink [drĭngk] **17** 2

drive [drīv] **97** 15

driveway [drīv/ wā/] **27** 1

drugstore [drŭg/ stör/] **45** 22

drum [drŭm] **98** 19

drummer [drŭm/ ər] **99** 27

drumsticks [drŭm/ stĭks/] **98** 19a

dry [drī] **25** 14, **38** 9

dryer [drī/ ər] **35** 24

duck [dŭk] **11** 25, **64** 25

(duck) pond [dŭk/ pŏnd/] **87** 8

dugout [dŭg/ owt/] **93** 13

dump truck [dŭmp/ trŭk/] **49** 14

dust [dŭst] **38** 15

dustpan [dŭst/ păn/] **35** 8

eagle [ē/ gəl] **64** 5

ear [ïr] **4** 34

(ear of) corn [ïr/ əv körn/] **6** 12

earmuffs [ïr/ mŭfs/] **19** 10

earrings [ïr/ ĭngz] **23** 1

Earth [ürth] **74** 8, **13**

east [ēst] **71** 73

East China Sea [ēst/ chī/ nə sē/] **70** 38

eat [ēt] **17** 1

eel [ēl] **65** 4

egg [ĕg] **18** 32, **64** 13

egg roll [ĕg/ rōl/] **18** 25

eggplant [ĕg/ plănt/] **7** 21

elbow [ĕl/ bō] **4** 8

electric drill [ĭ lĕk/ trĭk drĭl/] **37** 43

electric guitar [ĭ lĕk/ trĭk gĭ tär/] **99** 26

electric generator [ĭ lĕk/ trĭk gĕn/ ə rā tər] **80** 21

electrical tape [ĭ lĕk/ trĭ kəl tāp/] **37** 34

electrician [ĭ lĕk trī/ shən] **85** 6

electricity [ĭ lĕk trĭs/ ĭ tē] **80** 32

electronics [ĭ lĕk trŏn/ ĭks] **100**

elephant [ĕl/ ə fənt] **66** 17

elevator [ĕl/ ə vā/ tər] **45** 17, **80** 9

elm [ĕlm] **61** 36

embroidery [ĕm broi/ də rē] **101** 27

emergency brake [ĭ mür/ jən sē brāk/] **50** 15

emery board [ĕm/ ə rē börd/] **23** 24

encyclopedia [ĕn sī/ klə pē/ dē ə] **47** 25

end table [ĕnd/ tā/ bəl] **28** 29

end zone [ĕnd/ zōn/] **93** 23

energy [ĕn/ ər jē] **80**

engagement ring [ĕn gāj/ mənt rĭng/] **23** 3

engine [ĕn/ jən] **51, 52** 32

engineer [ĕn/ jə nïr/] **55** 15

enter [ĕn/ tər] **77** 14

entrance ramp [ĕn/ trəns rămp/] **53** 21

envelope [ĕn/ və lōp/] **46** 16, **83** 31

equator [ĭ kwā/ tər] **71** 70

erase [ĭ rās/] **77** 3

eraser [ĭ rā/ sər] **76** 11

escarole [ĕs/ kə rōl/] **6** 7

esophagus [ĭ sŏf/ ə gəs] **5** 61

eucalyptus [yōō/ kə lĭp/ təs] **61** 27

Europe [yōōr/ əp] **70** 3

examining table [ĭg zăm/ ə nĭng tā/ bəl] **39** 6

exhaust pipe [ĭg zöst/ pīp/] **52** 33

exit ramp [ĕg/ zĭt rămp/] **53** 2

exit sign [ĕg/ zĭt sīn/] **53** 24

Express Mail (package) [ĭk sprĕs/ māl păk/ ĭj] **46** 23

extension cord [ĭk stĕn/ shən körd/] **36** 5

eye [ī] **5**

eye drops [ī/ drŏps/] **41** 10

eye shadow [ī/ shă/ dō] **23** 30

eyebrow [ī/ brow/] **5** 44

eyebrow pencil [ī/ brow pĕn/ səl] **23** 26

eyelashes [ī/ lăsh/ əz] **5** 46

eyelid [ī/ lĭd/] **5** 45

eyeliner [ī/ lī/ nər] **23** 33

fabric softener [făb/ rĭk sö/ fə nər] **35** 27

face [fās] **4** 1

face guard [fās/ gärd/] **92** 15

factory work [făk/ tə rē würk/] **85**

fairway [fër/ wā/] **95** 12

fall [föl] **96** 7

Fall [föl] **26**

family [făm/ ə lē] **3**

family restaurant [făm/ ə lē rĕs/ tər ənt] **16**

fan belt [făn/ bĕlt/] **51** 53

fare [fër] **55** 21

fare box [fër/ bŏks/] **54** 5

farmhouse [färm/ hows/] **81** 3

farmer [fär/ mər] **81** 7

farming [fär/ mĭng] **81**

fashion designer [făsh/ ən də zī/ nər] **86** 6

father [fŏdh/ ər] **3** 5

faucet [fö/ sĭt] **34** 17, 18

fawn [fön] **67** 27

feather [fĕdh/ ər] **64** 7a

feather duster [fĕdh/ ər dŭs/ tər] **35** 2

fence [fĕns] **81** 9

fender [fĕn/ dər] **52** 10

ferry [fĕr/ ē] **58** 17

fever [fē/ vər] **40** 2

field [fēld] **81** 16

fields and courses [fēldz/ ənd kör/ səz] **95**

fig [fĭg] **9** 21

fighter plane [fī/ tər plān/] **48** 1

file cabinet [fīl/ kăb/ ə nət] **83** 21

file clerk [fīl/ klürk/] **83** 23

file folder [fīl/ fōl/ dər] **83** 22

filet [fĭ lā/] **11** 28

fill [fĭl] **26** 9

film [fĭlm] **100** 10, **100** 17

filter paper [fĭl/ tər pā/ pər] **78** 16

fin [fĭn] **65** 3b

finger [fĭng/ gər] **4** 25

fingernail [fĭng/ gər nāl/] **4** 23

fingerprints [fĭng/ gər prĭnts/] **43** 24

finish line [fĭn/ ĭsh līn/] **95** 21

fire [fīr] **28** 9, **42** 5

fire engine [fīr/ ĕn/ jən] **42** 2

fire escape [fīr/ ə skāp/] **42** 4

fire extinguisher [fīr/ ĭk stĭng/ gwĭ shər] **42** 11

fire fighter [fīr/ fī/ tər] **42** 10

fire hydrant [fīr/ hī/ drənt] **42** 9

fire truck [fīr/ trŭk/] **42** 3

firefighting [fīr/ fī/ tĭng] **42**

firefly [fīr/ flī/] **63** 17

fireplace [fīr′ plās′] **28** 8

first baseman [fürst′ bās′ mən] **93** 8

first quarter [fürst′ kwör′ tər] **74** 23

fish [fĭsh] **11** 26, **65**

fisherman [fĭsh′ ər mən] **58** 2

fishing [fĭsh′ ĭng] **88**

fishing boat [fĭsh′ ĭng bōt′] **58** 1

fishing line [fĭsh′ ĭng līn′] **88** 8

fishing net [fĭsh′ ĭng nĕt′] **88** 9

fishing rod [fĭsh′ ĭng rŏd′] **88** 7

flag [flăg] **76** 1, **82** 20, **95** 9

flame [flām] **29** 26, **78** 21

flamingo [flə mĭng′ gō] **64** 29

flanker [flăng′ kər] **93** 31

flannel shirt [flăn′ əl shürt′] **19** 3

flare [flër] **51** 41

flash [flăsh] **100** 7

flashlight [flăsh′ līt′] **35** 3

flask [flăsk] **78** 2

(flat) sheet [flăt′ shēt′] **32** 19

flatbed [flăt′ bĕd′] **49** 18

flight attendant [flīt′ ə tĕn′ dənt] **56** 20

flight deck [flīt′ dĕk′] **75** 10

flight engineer [flīt′ ĕn jə nïr′] **56** 17

flipper [flĭp′ ər] **68** 12a

flippers [flĭp′ ərz] **91** 36

floor [flör] **32** 29

Florida [flör′ ə də] **72** 9

florist [flör′ ĭst] **84** 11

flounder [flown′ dər] **65** 7

flowers [flow′ ərz] **60**

flute [flŏŏt] **99** 13

fly [flī] **63** 18

flying mammal [flī′ ĭng mă′ məlz] **66**

foal [fōl] **67** 22

foggy [fŏg′ ē] **25** 12

fold [fōld] **38** 1

food [fŏŏd] **6-18**

foot [fŏŏt] **5**

football [fŏŏt′ böl′] **92, 92** 13

football field [fŏŏt′ böl fēld′] **93**

forceps [för′ səps] **78** 28

forearm [för′ ärm′] **4** 9

forehead [för′ hĕd′] **4** 32

forelegs [för′ lĕgz′] **66** 3d

foreman [för′ mən] **85** 13

fork [förk] **29** 12

forklift [förk′ lĭft′] **58** 4

foul line [fowl′ līn′] **93** 9

foundation [fown dā′ shən] **82** 11

four-door hatchback [för′ dör hăch′ băk]
    51

fox [fŏks] **68** 6

fractions [frăk′ shənz] **79**

frame [frām] **28** 4

frame backpack [frām′ băk′ păk] **89** 28

freezer [frē′ zər] **14** 3, **30** 20

freezing [frē′ zĭng] **25** 11

french fries [frĕnch′ frīz′] **18** 28

French horn [frĕnch′ hörn′] **98** 26

fried chicken [frīd′ chĭk′ ən] **18** 29

Frisbee™ [frĭz′ bē] **90** 13

frog [frŏg] **65** 17

from [frŭm] **103** 10

front bumper [frŭnt′ bŭm′ pər] **51** 51

frozen foods [frō′zən fŏŏdz′] **14** 2

fruit and vegetable market
    [frŏŏt′ ənd vĕj′ tə bəl mär′ kət] **44** 28

fruit tree [frŏŏt′ trē′] **81** 2

fruits [frŏŏts] **8**

fry [frī] **31** 15

frying pan [frī′ ĭng păn′] **30** 5

fuel truck [fyŏŏ′ əl trŭk′] **49** 3

full moon [fŏŏl′ mŏŏn′] **74** 24

full slip [fŏŏl′ slĭp′] **22** 10

fullback [fŏŏl′ băk′] **93** 34

funnel [fŭn′ əl] **78** 17

fuselage [fyŏŏ′ sə lŏj′] **57** 14

galaxy [găl′ək sē] **74** 1

Ganges River [găn′ jēz rĭv′ər] **71** 67

gangway [găng′ wā′] **58** 20

garage [gə rŏj′] **27** 2

garbage can [gär′ bĭj kăn′] **35** 31

garbage truck [gär′ bĭj trŭk′] **49** 6

garden hose [gär′ dən hōs′] **27** 14

gardenia [gär dēn′ yə] **60** 14

gardener [gärd′ nər] **85** 3

garlic [gär′ lĭk] **7** 25

garment bag [gär′ mənt băg′] **56** 1

garter belt [gär′ tər bĕlt′] **22** 14

(garter) snake [gär′ tər snāk′] **65** 9

gas gauge [găs′ gāj′] **50** 9

gas pump [găs′ pŭmp′] **53** 14

gas tank [găs′ tăngk′] **50** 34

gas(oline) [găs′ ə lēn′] **80** 28

(gauze) bandage [göz′ băn′ dĭj] **39** 24

gauze pads [göz′ pădz′] **39** 25

gavel [găv′ əl] **43** 12

gear [gïr] **89** 27

gear changer [gïr′ chān′ jər] **52** 22

gearshift [gïr′ shĭft′] **50** 17

geometrical figures
    [jē′ ə mĕ′ trĭ kəl fĭg′ yərz] **79**

Georgia [jör′ jə] **72** 10

geyser [gī′ zər] **80** 5

gibbon [gĭb′ ən] **69** 15

gill [gĭl] **65** 3c

giraffe [jə răf′] **67** 29

girdle [gür′ dəl] **22** 15

girl [gürl] **2** 9

girl's frame [gürlz′ frām′] **52** 3

give [gĭv] **17** 9

glass [glăs] **12** 20

glasses [glăs′ əz] **21** 44

glider [glī′ dər] **57** 4

globe [glōb] **47** 19

glove [glŭv] **92** 12, **94** 11, **94** 15

glove compartment
    [glŭv′ kəm pärt′ mənt] **50** 20

gloves [glŭvz] **19** 1

glue [glŏŏ] **36** 33, **76** 17

goal [gōl] **92** 25

goalie [gōl′ ē] **92** 24

goalpost [gōl′ pōst′] **93** 35

goat [gōt] **67** 28

Gobi Desert [gō′ bē dĕz′ ərt] **71** 54

golf [gŏlf] **94**

golf bag [gŏlf′ băg′] **95** 7

golf ball [gŏlf′ böl′] **94** 7

golf cart [gŏlf′ kärt′] **95** 8

golf course [gŏlf′ körs′] **95**

golfer [gŏl′ fər] **94** 10

goose [gŏŏs] **64** 26

gooseberries [gŏŏs′ bĕr′ ēz] **8** 11

gopher [gō′ fər] **66** 8

gorilla [gə rĭl′ ə] **69** 17

graduated cylinder
    [grăj′ ŏŏ ā tĭd sĭl′ ən dər] **78** 25

grains [grānz] **60**

granddaughter [grănd′ dö′ tər] **2** 11

grandfather [grănd′ fŏ′ dhər] **3** 2

grandmother [grănd′ mŭ′ dhər] **3** 1

grandparents [grănd păr′ ənts] **2** 10

grandson [grănd′ sŭn′] **2** 12

grapefruit [grăp′ frōōt′] **8** 7

grapes [grāps] **8** 1

graph paper [grăf′ pā′ pər] **78** 11

grass [grăs] **27** 15

grasses [grăs′ əz] **60**

grasshopper [grăs′ hŏp′ ər] **63** 6

grate [grāt] **31** 2

Great Sandy Desert
  [grāt′ săn′ dē dĕz′ ərt] **71** 55

green [grēn] **95** 10

greengrocer [grēn′ grō′ sər] **84** 7

grill [grĭl] **27** 22, **88** 12

grizzly bear [grĭz′ lē bër′] **69** 23

groceries [grō′ sə rēz] **15** 24

ground beef [grownd′ bēf′] **10** 2

grounding plug [grown′ dĭng plŭg′]
  36 7

guitar [gĭ tär′] **98** 11

Gulf of Alaska [gŭlf′ əv ə lăs′ kə]
  70 17

Gulf of Guinea [gŭlf′ əv gĭn′ ē] **70** 25

Gulf of Mexico [gŭlf′ əv mĕk sə kō]
  70 19

gulfs [gŭlfs] **70**

gun [gŭn] **43** 7

gun turret [gŭn′ tür′ ət] **48** 12

gutter [gŭt′ ər] **27** 10, **94** 3

gymnast [jĭm′ năst] **94** 23

gymnastics [jĭm năs′ tĭks] **94**

hacksaw [hăk′ sö′] **36** 18

hair [hër] **4** 30

hair dryer [hër′ drī′ ər] **34** 26

hairbrush [hër′ brŭsh′] **32** 7

hairdresser [hër′ drĕs′ ər] **84** 10

half (1/2) [hăf] **79** 30

half slip [hăf′ slĭp′] **22** 8

halfback [hăf′ băk′] **93** 33

hall [höl] **76** 12

ham [hăm] **10** 12

hamburger [hăm′bür′ gər] **18** 9

hammer [hăm′ ər] **36** 13

hammock [hăm′ ək] **27** 11

hamper [hăm′ pər] **34** 28

hand [hănd] **4**

hand brake [hănd′ brāk′] **52** 24

hand grenade [hănd′ grə nād′] **48** 29

hand towel [hănd′ tow′ əl] **34** 23

hand truck [hănd′ trŭk′] **87** 4

handball [hănd′ böl′] **94, 94** 12

handcuffs [hănd′ kŭfs′] **43** 4

handicrafts [hăn′ dē krăfts′] **101**

handlebars [hăn′ dəl bärz′] **52** 2

hang [hăng] **38** 6

hang glider [hăng′ glī′ dər] **57** 6

hangar [hăng′ ər] **57** 17

hanger [hăng′ ər] **32** 2

hard hat [härd′ hăt′] **21** 28, **82** 4

harmonica [här mŏn′ ə kə] **98** 30

harness [här′ nəs] **89** 22

harp [härp] **98** 6

hat [hăt] **19** 18

hatchback [hăch′ băk′] **51** 43

hatchet [hăch′ ət] **36** 17

Hawaii [hə wŏ′ ē] **72** 11

hawk [hök] **64** 7

hay [hā] **81** 13

hazelnut(s) [hā′ zəl nŭt(s)′] **9** 30

head [hĕd] **4, 36** 42a

(head of) cauliflower
  [hĕd′ əv kŏl ə flow′ ər] **6** 1

head protector [hĕd prə tĕk′ tər] **94** 14

headache [hĕd′ āk′] **40** 6

headboard [hĕd′ börd′] **32** 14

headlights [hĕd′ līts′] **51** 48

headphones [hĕd′ fōnz′] **100** 29

headrest [hĕd′ rĕst′] **50** 35

headset [hĕd′ sĕt′] **83** 2

heart [härt] **5** 64

heat [hēt] **80** 27

heating pad [hē′ tĭng păd′] **41** 3

hedge clippers [hĕj′ klĭp′ ərz] **27** 29

heel [hēl] **5** 50, **20** 5

heels [hēlz] **20** 25

height [hīt] **79** 34

helicopter [hĕl′ ə kŏp′ tər] **57** 2

helmet [hĕl′ mət] **42** 12, **52** 7, **92** 14

hem [hĕm] **101** 11

hem binding [hĕm′ bīn′ dĭng] **101** 12

herb(s) [ürb(z)] **6** 9

(herd of) cattle [hürd′ əv kăt′ əl] **81** 20

high [hī] **24** 11

high blood pressure [hī′ blŭd prĕsh′ ər]
  40 10

high chair [hī′ chër′] **16** 8

high heels [hī′ hēlz′] **20** 25

highway travel [hī′ wā trăv′ əl] **53**

hikers [hī′ kərz] **88** 2

hiking boots [hī′ kĭng bōōts′] **19** 9

hill [hĭl] **88** 4

Himalayas [hĭm′ ə lā′ əz] **70** 47

hind legs [hīnd′ lĕgz′] **66** 3b

hip [hĭp] **4** 16

hippopotamus [hĭp′ ə pŏt′ ə məs]
  66 14

hit [hĭt] **96** 1

hitchhiker [hĭch′ hī′ kər] **53** 9

hockey stick [hŏk′ ē stĭk′] **92** 18

hog [hög] **66** 30

hold [hōld] **17** 12, **58** 8

hole [hōl] **94** 8

holly [hŏl′ ē] **61** 37

holster [hōl′ stər] **43** 8

home plate [hōm′ plāt′] **93** 15

honeydew melon
  [hŭn′ ē dōō mĕl′ ən] **9** 35

hood [hōōd] **51** 47

hoof [hōōf] **66** 35b

hoofed mammals [hōōft′ măm′ əlz] **66**

hook [hōōk] **32** 1, **36** 16

hook and eye [hōōk′ ənd ī′] **101** 14

horn [hörn] **50** 12, **52** 5, **66** 16a

horse [hörs] **66** 21

horse racing [hörs′ rā′ sĭng] **94**

horse-drawn carriage
  [hörs′ drön kăr′ ij] **54** 33

horseback rider [hörs′ băk rī′ dər]
  87 6

horses [hörs′ əz] **81** 23

hose [hōz] **42** 8, **50** 57

hot [hŏt] **25** 7

hot air balloon [hŏt′ ër bə lōōn′] **57** 1

hot dog [hŏt′ dög′] **18** 2

hot water faucet [hŏt′ wŏt ər fö′ sət]
  34 17

house plants [hows′ plănts′] **60** 39

household items [hows′ hōld ī′ təmz]
  15 15

household services
  [hows′ hōld sür′ və səz] **85**

housekeeper [hows′ kē′ pər] **85** 8

houses [how′ zəz] **27**

housework [hows′ würk′] **38**

Huang River [hwŏng′ riv′ ər] **71** 68

hubcap [hŭb′ kăp′] **50** 36

Hudson Bay [hŭd′ sən bā′] **70** 18
human body [hyōō′ mən bŏd′ ē] **4**
hummingbird [hŭm′ ĭng bürd′] **64** 2
hump [hŭmp] **67** 33a
husband [hŭz′ bənd] **2** 3, **3** 12
hyacinth [hī′ ə sĭnth] **60** 10
hyena [hī ē′ nə] **68** 30
hypotenuse [hī pŏt′ ə nōōs′] **79** 24
ice cream cone [īs′ krēm cōn′] **18** 36
ice hockey [īs′ hŏk′ ē] **92**
ice pack [īs′ păk′] **41** 4
ice skates [īs′ skāts′] **19** 15
ice skating [īs′ skā′ tĭng] **94**
ice tray [īs′ trā′] **30** 21
icy [ī′ sē] **25** 16
Idaho [ī′ də hō′] **72** 12
ignition [ĭg nĭsh′ ən] **50** 14
iguana [ĭ gwŏ′ nə] **65** 13
Illinois [ĭl′ ə noy′] **72** 13
in [ĭn] **102** 7
in front of [ĭn frŭnt′ əv] **102** 6
in-box [ĭn′ bŏks] **83** 12
(index) finger [ĭn′ dĕks fing′ gər] **4** 25
Indian Ocean [ĭn′ dē ən ō′ shən′] **70** 13
Indiana [ĭn′ dē ăn′ ə] **72** 14
individual sports
    [ĭn′ də vĭj′ ōō əl spörts′] **94**
infection [ĭn fĕk′ shən] **40** 14
inflatable raft [ĭn flā′ tə bəl răft′] **59** 20
information desk
    [ĭn′ fər mā′ shən dĕsk′] **47** 22
injection [ĭn jĕk′ shən] **41** 8
injuries [ĭn′ jə rēz] **40**
insect bite [ĭn′ sĕkt bīt′] **40** 3
insects [ĭn′ sĕkts] **63**
instep [ĭn′ stĕp′] **5** 51
instruments [ĭn′ strə mənts]
    39 13, **56** 14, **98**
internal organs [ĭn tür′ nəl ör′ gənz] **5**
intersection [ĭn′ tər sĕk′ shən] **44** 11
interstate highway
    [ĭn′ tər stāt hī′ wā] **53** 1
intestines [ĭn tĕs′ tənz] **5** 67
into [ĭn′ tōō] **103** 12
Iowa [ī′ ə wə] **72** 15
iris [ī′ rəs] **5** 47, **60** 11
iron (n) [ī′ ərn] **35** 12
iron (v) [ī′ ərn] **38** 11

ironing board [ī′ ər nĭng börd′] **35** 13
jack [jăk] **32** 26b, **50** 38
jacket [jăk′ ət] **19** 17, **21** 33
jackhammer [jăk′ hăm′ər] **82** 22
jail [jāl] **43** 1
janitor [jăn′ ə tər] **85** 9
jar [jär] **12** 9
jaw [jö] **4** 38
jeans [jēnz] **19** 6
jeep [jēp] **48** 9
jelly [jĕl′ ē] **18** 31
jellyfish [jĕl′ ē fĭsh′] **62** 12
jet engine [jĕt′ ĕn′ jən] **57** 11
jet fuel [jĕt′ fyōō′ əl] **80** 31
(jet) plane [jĕt′ plān′] **57** 18
jeweller [jōō′ ə lər] **84** 12
jewelry [jōō′ əl rē] **23**
jewelry box [jōō′ əl rē bŏks′] **32** 4
jigsaw [jĭg′ sö] **36** 3
jockey [jŏk′ ē] **94** 21
jogging path [jŏg′ ĭng păth′] **87** 9
judge [jŭj] **43** 10
jukebox [jōōk′ bŏks′] **16** 12
jump [jŭmp] **96** 8
jungle gym [jŭng′ əl jĭm′] **87** 17
Jupiter [jōō′ pə tər] **74** 15
jury [jōōr′ ē] **43** 21
jury box [joor′ ē bŏks′] **43** 20
kangaroo [kăng′ gə rōō′] **66** 3
Kansas [kăn′ zəs] **72** 16
Kara Sea [kär′ ə sē′] **70** 31
kayak [kī′ ăk] **59** 17
Kentucky [kĕn tŭk′ ē] **72** 17
ketchup [kĕch′ əp] **16** 4
kettledrum [kĕt′ əl drŭm′] **98** 21
keyboard [kē′ börd] **98** 1a, **100** 33
keyboard player [kē′ börd plā′ ər] **99** 22
kickstand [kĭk′ stănd′] **52** 9
kidney [kĭd′ nē] **5** 70
kidney bean(s) [kĭd′ nē bēn(z)′] **6** 13
kitchen [kĭch′ ən] **30**
kite [kīt] **91** 22
kitten [kĭt′ ən] **68** 5
knee [nē] **4** 19
knee socks [nē′ sŏks′] **22** 16
knife [nīf] **29** 15
knitting [nĭt′ ĭng] **101** 22
knitting needle [nĭt′ ĭng nē′ dəl] **101** 25

knuckle [nŭk′ əl] **4** 22
koala [kō ŏl′ ə] **66** 1
label [lā′ bəl] **46** 21
lacrosse [lə krös′] **92**
lacrosse stick [lə krös′ stĭk′] **92** 16
ladder [lăd′ ər] **42** 1, **82** 8
ladybug [lā′ dē bŭg′] **63** 14
lamb [lăm] **10** 13, **67** 24
lamp [lămp] **28** 28
lampshade [lămp′ shād′] **28** 27
landing gear [lăn′ dĭng gïr′] **57** 15
lane [lān] **94** 4
lantern [lăn′ tərn] **88** 29
lapel [lə pĕl′] **20** 1
Laptev Sea [lăp′ tĕv sē′] **70** 33
last quarter [lăst′ kwör′ tər] **74** 25
launchpad [lönch′ păd′] **75** 15
laundry [lön′ drē] **35** 28
laundry basket [lön′ drē băs′ kət] **35** 29
laundry detergent [lön′ drē də tür′ jənt]
    35 25
lawn mower [lön′ mō′ ər] **27** 12
lead guitarist [lēd′ gĭ tär′ ĭst] **99** 25
leaf [lēf] **60** 36a
leave [lēv] **77** 13
left fielder [lĕft′ fēl′ dər] **93** 1
left guard [lĕft′ gärd′] **93** 26
left lane [lĕft′ lān′] **53** 5
left tackle [lĕft′ tăk′ əl] **93** 25
leg [lĕg] **4** 17, **10** 14, **11** 20
(legal) pad [lē′ gəl păd′] **83** 26
lemon [lĕm′ ən] **8** 9
Lena River [lē′ nə rĭv′ ər] **71** 66
length [lĕngth] **79** 36
lens [lĕnz] **100** 6
leopard [lĕp′ ərd] **68** 1
letter [lĕt′ ər] **46** 7
letter carrier [lĕt′ ər kăr′ yər] **46** 3
lettuce [lĕt′ əs] **6** 6
level [lĕv′ əl] **82** 3
librarian [lī brër′ ē ən] **47** 23
library card [lī′ brër ē kärd′] **47** 3
library clerk [lī′ brër ē klürk′] **47** 1
license plate [lī′ səns plāt′] **50** 28
lid [lĭd] **30** 9
life jacket [līf′ jăk′ ət] **59** 1
life preserver [līf′ prə zür′ vər] **90** 9
lifeboat [līf′ bōt′] **58** 19, **90** 10

lifeguard [līf′ gärd′] **90** 6

lifeguard chair [līf′ gärd chër′] **90** 8

light (*v*) [līt] **17** 13

light (*adj*) [līt] **24** 9

light switch [līt′ swĭch′] **32** 25

lightbulb [līt′ bŭlb′] **35** 22

lighter [lī′ tər] **16** 30

lighthouse [līt′ hows′] **58** 14

lily [lĭl′ ē] **60** 3

lima bean(s) [lī′ mə bēn(z)′] **6** 16

lime [līm] **8** 10

line [līn] **58** 25

lines [līnz] **79**

linesman [līnz′ mən] **82** 17

lion [lī′ ən] **68** 3

lip [lĭp] **4** 43

lipstick [lĭp′ stĭk′] **23** 29

liquor (bottle) [lĭk′ ər bŏt′ əl] **16** 22

listen [lĭs′ ən] **77** 6

little finger [lĭt′ əl fĭng′ gər] **4** 28

little league baseball [lĭt′ əl lēg bās′ böl]
    92

Little Leaguer [lĭt′ əl lēg′ ər] **92** 8

little toe [lĭt′ əl tō′] **5** 55

liver [lĭv′ ər] **5** 65

livestock [līv′ stŏk′] **81** 12

living quarters [lĭv′ ĭng kwör′ tərz]
    75 11

living room [lĭv′ ĭng rōōm′] **28**

lizard [lĭz′ ərd] **65** 15

llama [lŏm′ ə] **66** 15

loaf [lōf] **12** 7

loafer [lō′ fər] **21** 42

lobby [lŏb′ ē] **44** 2

lobster [lŏb′ stər] **10** 30, **62** 13

lock [lŏk] **52** 13

locker [lŏk′ ər] **76** 6

locksmith [lŏk′ smĭth′] **85** 4

log [lög] **28** 10

long [löng] **24** 2

long johns [löng′ jŏnz′] **22** 7

long sleeve [löng′ slēv′] **20** 15

loose [lōōs] **24** 4

(loose-leaf) paper [lōōs′ lēf pā′ pər]
    76 13

loudspeaker [lowd′ spē′ kər] **76** 3

Louisiana [lōō ē′ zē ăn′ ə] **72** 18

lounge chair [lownj′ chër′] **27** 24

low [lō] **24** 12

lunar eclipse [lōō′ nər ĭ klĭps′] **74** 6

lunar module [lōō′ nər mŏj′ ōōl] **75** 7

lunch box [lŭnch′ bŏks′] **20** 31

lunch truck [lŭnch′ trŭk′] **49** 8

lung [lŭng] **5** 63

machine gun [mə shēn′ gŭn′] **48** 25

magazine [măg′ ə zēn′] **47** 16

magnet [măg′ nət] **78** 27

magnifying glass [măg′ nə fī ĭng glăs′]
    78 15

magnolia [măg nōl′ yə] **61** 29

mail [māl] **46** 2

mail slot [māl′ slŏt′] **46** 13

mail truck [māl′ trŭk′] **46** 5

mailbag [māl′ băg′] **46** 4

mailbox [māl′ bŏks′] **46** 1

Maine [mān] **72** 19

maintenance [mān′ tə nəns] **95**

make (the bed) [māk′ dhə bĕd′] **38** 8

makeup [māk′ ŭp′] **23**

mallet [măl′ ĭt] **36** 11

mammals [măm′ əlz] **66-69**

man [măn] **2** 2

manager [măn′ ĭ jər] **83** 18

mandolin [măn′ də lĭn′] **98** 4

mane [mān] **66** 21a

mango [măng′ gō] **8** 5

manhole [măn′ hōl′] **45** 32

mantel [măn′ təl] **28** 7

mantis [măn′ tĭs] **63** 7

manual transmission
    [măn′ yōō əl trănz mĭsh′ ən] **50**

map [măp] **70**

maple [mā′ pəl] **61** 38

marigold [măr′ ə gōld′] **60** 6

marine [mə rēn′] **48** 18

Marines [mə rēnz′] **48** 17

Mars [märz] **74** 14

Maryland [mër′ ə lənd] **72** 20

mascara [mă skăr′ ə] **23** 28

mashed potatoes [măsht′ pə tā tōz′]
    18 17

mask [măsk] **91** 35

Massachusetts [măs′ ə chōō′ sĭts]
    72 21

mast [măst] **59** 8

mat [măt] **50** 22

matches [măch′ əz] **16** 28

material [mə tïr′ ē əl] **101** 4

math [măth] **79**

mattress [mă′ trəs] **32** 17

measurement [mĕzh′ ər mənt] **79**

meat [mēt] **10**

meatballs [mēt′ bölz′] **18** 11

mechanic [mə kăn′ ĭk] **84** 2

media [mē′ dē ə] **86**

medical care [mĕd′ ə kəl kër′] **39**

medicine [mĕd′ ə sən] **41**

medicine chest [mĕd′ ə sən chĕst′]
    34 14

medicine dropper [mĕd′ ə sən drŏp′ ər]
    78 26

Mediterranean Sea
    [mĕd′ ĭ tə rā′ nē ən sē′] **70** 24

melon [mĕl′ ən] **9** 35

menu [mĕn′ yōō] **16** 7

Mercury [mür′ kyə rē] **74** 11

merry-go-round [mër′ ē gō rownd′]
    87 5

message pad [mĕs′ ĭj păd′] **83** 25

messenger [mĕs′ ən jər] **86** 19

metal detector [mĕt′ əl də tĕk′ tər]
    56 10

meteor [mē′ tē ər] **74** 5

meter [mē′ tər] **55** 23

mezzanine [mĕz′ ə nēn′] **99** 13

Michigan [mĭsh′ ə gən] **72** 22

microfilm [mī′ krə fĭlm′] **47** 13

microfilm reader [mī′ krə fĭlm rē′ dər]
    47 14

microscope [mī′ krə skōp′] **78** 30

microwave oven [mī′ krə wāv ŭv′ ən]
    30 23

middle finger [mĭd′ əl fĭng′ gər] **4** 26

milk [mĭlk] **14** 5

Minicam™ [mĭn′ ē kăm′] **100** 2

Minnesota [mĭn′ ə sō′ tə] **72** 23

mirror [mïr′ ər] **32** 5

Mississippi [mĭs′ ə sĭp′ ē] **72** 24

Mississippi River [mĭs′ ə sĭp′ ē rĭv′ ər]
    71 58

Missouri [mĭ zŏŏr′ ē] **73** 25

mitt [mĭt] **27** 20

mittens [mĭt′ ənz] **19** 11

mixed vegetables [mǐkst′ věj′ tə bəlz] **18** 16

mixing bowl [mǐk′ sǐng bōl′] **30** 24

mobile [mō′ bēl] **33** 2

model [mǒd′ əl] **86** 5

Mojave Desert [mō hǒv′ ē děz′ ərt] **71** 48

money [mǔn′ ē] **12**

money order [mǔn′ ē ör′ dər] **46** 18

monitor [mǒn′ ə tər] **100** 32

monkey [mǔng′ ke] **69** 14

monkey wrench [mǔng′ kē rěnch′] **36** 12

monorail [mǒn′ ə rāl′] **55** 29

Montana [mǒn tǎn′ ə] **73** 26

Moon [mōōn] **74** 9

mooring [mōōr′ ǐng] **59** 19

moose [mōōs] **67** 35

mop [mǒp] **35** 6

(mop) refill [mǒp′ rē′ fǐl] **35** 11

mortar [mör′ tər] **48** 28

mosquito [mə skē′ tō] **63** 13

motel [mō těl′] **90** 3

moth [mǒth] **63** 21

mother [mǔdh′ ər] **3** 4

motor oil [mōt′ər oyl′] **80** 33

motor scooter [mōt′ ər skōō′ tər] **52** 29

motorboat [mōt′ ər bōt′] **59** 13

motorcycle [mōt′ər sī′ kəl] **52** 30, **53** 19

mountain [mown′ tən] **89** 19

mountain climbing [mown′ tən klīm′ ǐng] **89**

mountain ranges [mown′ tən rān′ jəz] **71**

mouse [mows] **66** 9

mousetrap [mows′ trǎp′] **35** 32

mouth [mowth] **4** 2

mover [mōō′ vər] **49** 12

movie camera [mōō′ vē kǎm′ ə rə] **100** 15

moving van [mōō′ vǐng vǎn′] **49** 11

mow [mō] **26** 6

mum [mǔm] **60** 4

muscle [mǔs′ əl] **5** 62

mushroom(s) [mǔsh′ rōōm(z)] **7** 30

music [myōō′ zǐk] **99**

musical comedy [myōō′ zə kəl kǒm′ ə dē] **99**

musical instruments [myōō′ zə kəl ǐn′ strə mənts] **98**

musician [myōō zǐsh′ ən] **99** 10

mussel(s) [mǔs′ əl(z)] **11** 34, **62** 3

mustache [mǔs′ tǎsh] **4** 40

mustard [mǔs′ tərd] **18** 1

nail [nāl] **37** 41

nail clippers [nāl′ klǐp′ ərz] **23** 31

nail polish [nāl′ pǒl′ ǐsh] **23** 25

nailbrush [nāl′ brǔsh′] **34** 20

napkin [nǎp′ kǐn] **29** 14

natural gas [nǎch′ ər əl gǎs′] **80** 29

Navy [nā′ vē] **48** 13

Nebraska [nə brǎs′ kə] **73** 27

neck [něk] **4** 4

necklace [něk′ lǐs] **23** 6

nectarine [něk′ tə rēn′] **8** 17

needle [nē′ dəl] **39** 26, **60** 34a, **101** 18

needlecrafts [nē′ dəl krǎfts′] **101**

needlepoint [nē′ dəl poynt′] **101** 26

neighborhood parks [nā′ bər hōod pärks′] **87**

nephew [něf′ yōō] **3** 13

Neptune [něp′ tōōn] **74** 18

nest [něst] **64** 31

net [nět] **92** 23

Nevada [nə vǎd′ ə] **73** 28

new [nōō] **24** 13

New Hampshire [nōō′ hǎmp′ shər] **72** 29

New Jersey [nōō′ jür′ ze] **73** 30

New Mexico [nōō′ měk′ sə kō] **73** 31

new moon [nōō′ mōōn′] **74** 26

New York [nōō′ yörk′] **73** 32

newscaster [nōōz′ kǎs′ tər] **86** 2

newspaper [nōōz′ pā′ pər] **21** 48

newsstand [nōōz′ stǎnd′] **45** 30

next to [někst′ tōō] **102** 11

nickel [nǐk′ əl] **13** 28

niece [nēs] **3** 14

Niger River [nī′ jər rǐv′ ər] **71** 61

night table [nīt′ tā′ bəl] **32** 27

nightgown [nīt′ gown′] **22** 21

nightstick [nīt′ stǐk′] **43** 9

Nile River [nīl′ rǐv′ ər] **71** 63

nipple [nǐp′ əl] **33** 18

north [nörth] **71** 71

North America [nörth′ ə mër′ ə kə] **70** 1

North Atlantic [nörth′ ăt lăn′ tǐk] **70** 11

North Carolina [nörth′ kǎr ə lī′ nə] **73** 33

North Dakota [nörth′ də kō′ tə] **73** 34

North Pacific [nörth′ pə sǐf′ ǐk] **70** 9

North Sea [nörth′ sē′] **70** 21

nose [nōz] **4** 36, **57** 8

nostril [nǒs′ trǐl] **4** 37

nozzle [nǒz′ əl] **42** 17

nuclear reactor [nōō′ klē ər rē ǎk′ tər] **80** 13

nurse [nürs] **39** 19

nut [nǔt] **37** 39

nuts [nǔts] **9**

oak [ōk] **61** 33

oar [ör] **59** 22

oarlock [ör′ lǒk′] **59** 21

oats [ōts] **60** 23

Ob River [ǒb′ rǐv′ ər] **71** 64

oboe [ō′ bō] **98** 15

obtuse angle [ǒb tōōs′ ǎng′ gəl] **79** 5

occupations [ǒk′ yə pā′ shənz] **84-86**

ocean liner [ō′ shən lī′ nər] **58** 27

oceans [ō′ shənz] **70**

octopus [ōk′ tə pəs] **62** 6

office [ö′ fǐs] **83**

office building [ö′ fǐs bǐl′ dǐng] **44** 1

officer [ö′ fǐ sər] **86** 13

Ohio [ō hī′ ō] **73** 35

oil [oyl] **38** 12

oil well [oyl′ wěl′] **80** 1

ointment [oynt′ mənt] **41** 9

Oklahoma [ō′ klə hō′ mə] **73** 36

old [ōld] **24** 14

on [ǒn] **102** 5

on top of [ǒn tǒp′ əv] **102** 10

onion(s) [ǔn′ yən(z)] **7** 31

open [ō′ pən] **24** 15, **31** 3

optician [ǒp tǐsh′ ən] **84** 9

oral hygienist [ör′ əl hī jē′ nǐst] **39** 14

orange [ör′ ǐnj] **8** 8

orangutan [ə rǎng′ ə tǎn′] **69** 18

orbit [ör′ bǐt] **74** 21

orchard [ör′ chərd] **81** 1

orchestra [ör′ kə strə] **99** 6

orchestra seating [ör′ kə strə sēt′ ĭng]
    99 12

orchid [ör′ kĭd] **60** 12

order [ör′ dər] **17** 5

Oregon [ör′ ə gən] **73** 37

organ [ör′ gən] **98** 29

ostrich [ŏs′ trĭch] **64** 12

otter [ŏt′ ər] **68** 10

out of [owt′ əv] **103** 7

outboard motor [owt′ börd mō′ tər]
    59 12

outer space [owt′ər spās′] **74**

outlet [owt′ lət] **36** 6

oval [ō′ vəl] **79** 18

oven [ŭv′ ən] **30** 32

over [ō′ vər] **103** 8

overalls [ō′ vər ölz′] **21** 30

overcoat [ō′ vər kōt′] **19** 20

overhead projector
    [ō′ vər hĕd prə jĕk′ tər] **76** 27

overpass [ō′ vər păs′] **53** 3

owl [owl] **64** 6

oyster(s) [oy′ stər(z)] **11** 33, **62** 2

pacifier [păs′ ə fĭ′ ər] **33** 22

pack [păk] **13** 16

package [păk′ ĭj] **12** 4, **46** 19

pad [păd] **83** 26

paddle [păd′ əl] **59** 3, **94** 18

pail [pāl] **90** 16

paint (v) [pānt] **26** 1

paint (n) [pānt] **37** 31

paintbrush [pānt′ brŭsh′] **37** 30

Painted Desert [pān′ təd dez′ ərt] **71** 49

painter [pān′ tər] **85** 7

painting [pān′ tĭng] **28** 5

(pair of) scissors [pĕr′ əv sĭz′ ərz]
    101 17

pajamas [pə jŏm′ əz] **22** 19

palm [pŏm] **4** 29, **61** 26

pan [păn] **37** 28

pancakes [păn′ kāks′] **18** 5

pancreas [pang′ krē əs] **5** 71

panda [păn də] **69** 20

panel truck [păn′ əl trŭk′] **49** 9

pansy [păn′ zē] **60** 2

panties [păn′ tēz] **22** 11

pants [pănts] **21** 27

pantyhose [păn′ tē hōz′] **22** 5

papaya [pə pī′ yə] **8** 6

paper [pā′ pər] **76** 13

paper clips [pā′ pər klĭps′] **83** 28

paper towels [pā′ pər tow′əlz] **35** 23

parachute [păr′ ə shoot′] **48** 6

parakeet [păr′ ə kēt] **64** 15

parallel lines [păr′ ə lĕl līnz′] **79** 4

paramedic [păr′ ə mĕd′ ĭk] **42** 7

Parana River [păr′ ə nŏ′ rĭv′ ər] **71** 60

parents [păr′ ənts] **2** 6

park [pärk] **87**

park ranger [pärk′ rān′ jər] **88** 5

parka [pär′ kə] **19** 8

parking lights [pär′ kĭng līts′] **51** 49

parking garage [pär′ kĭng gə rŏj′]
    45 19

parking meter [pär′ kĭng mē′ tər]
    45 20

parrot [păr′ ət] **64** 16

part [pärt] **4** 31

pass [păs] **96** 5

passenger [păs′ ĭn jər] **55** 25

passenger car [păs′ ĭn jər kär′] **53** 15

pasture [păs′ chər] **81** 6

patient [pā ′shənt] **39** 20

patio [păt′ ē ō′] **27** 17

pattern [păt ′ərn] **101** 7

pattern piece [păt′ ərn pēs′] **101** 6

paw [pö] **69** 29a

pay [pā] **17** 7

pea(s) [pē(z)] **6** 17

peach [pēch] **9** 37

peacock [pē′ kŏk′] **64** 18

peak [pēk] **89** 20

peanut(s) [pē′ nŭt(s)′] **9** 28

pear [pĕr] **8** 18

pedal [pĕd′ əl] **39** 18, **52** 19

pedestrian [pə dĕs′ trē ən] **44** 12

peel (n) [pēl] **9** 20a

peel (v) [pēl] **31** 5

pegboard [pĕg′ börd′] **36** 15

pelican [pĕl′ ə kən] **64** 24

pencil [pĕn′ səl] **76** 24

pencil eraser [pĕn′ səl ə rā′ sər] **76** 21

pencil sharpener
    [pĕn′ səl shär′ pə nər] **76** 20, **83** 30

Pennsylvania [pĕn səl vān′ yə] **73** 38

penny [pĕn′ ē] **13** 27

penguin [pĕn′ gwĭn] **64** 27

people [pē′ pəl] **2**

pepper shaker [pĕp′ ər shā′ kər] **29** 9

pepper(s) [pĕp′ ər(z)] **7** 22

percussion [pər kŭsh′ ən] **98**

perfume [pür′ fyoom] **23** 27

periodicals section
    [pĭr′ ē ŏd′ ə kəlz sĕk′ shən] **47** 15

periscope [pĕr′ə skōp′] **48** 8

perpendicular lines
    [pür′ pən dĭk′ yə lər līnz′] **79** 2

Persian Gulf [pür′ zhən gŭlf ′] **70** 28

personal computer (PC)
    [pür′ sə nəl kŭm pyoo′ tər]/
    [pē′ sē′] **100** 31

personnel [pür ′ sə nĕl′] **48**

petal [pĕt′ əl] **60** 18b

petri dish [pĕt′ rē dĭsh′] **78** 3

petunia [pə toon′ yə] **60** 7

pharmacist [fär′ mə sĭst] **84** 1

phases of the moon
    [fā′ zəz əv dhə moon′] **74**

pheasant [fĕz′ ənt] **64** 19

Phillips screwdriver
    [fĭl′ ĭps skroo′ drī vər] **37** 25

phone [fōn] **32** 26

photocopier [fō′ tə kŏp′ ē ər] **83** 24

photocopy machine
    [fō tə kŏp ē mə shēn′] **47** 18

photographer [fə tŏg′ rə fər] **86** 4

photography [fə tŏg′ rə fē] **100**

piano [pē ăn′ ō] **98** 1

piccolo [pĭk′ ə lō′] **98** 12

pick (v) [pĭk] **26** 7

pick (n) [pĭk] **98** 11a

pickup truck [pĭk′ ŭp trŭk′] **49** 4

pickax [pĭk′ ăks′] **82** 13

pickle [pĭk′ əl] **18** 8

picnic area [pĭk′nĭk ĕr′ ē ə] **88**

picnic basket [pĭk′ nĭk băs′ kət] **88** 13

picnic table [pĭk′ nĭk tā′ bəl] **88** 15

piece [pēs] **12** 22

pier [pĭr] **58** 3

pierced earring [pĭrst′ ĭr′ ĭng] **23** 16

pigeon [pĭj′ ən] **64** 1

pill [pĭl] **41** 7

pillow [pĭl′ ō] **32** 16

pillowcase [pĭl′ ō kās′] **32** 15

pilot [pī′ lət] **56** 15

pin [pĭn] **23** 8, **94** 5, **101** 20

pincushion [pĭn′ kŏŏsh′ ən] **101** 3

pine [pīn] **60** 34

pineapple [pīn′ ăp′ əl] **8** 4

ping-pong [pĭng′ pŏng′] **94**

ping-pong ball [pĭng′ pŏng böl′] **94** 19

pinking shears [pĭng′ kĭng shïrz′]
      101 5

pipe [pīp] **16** 26, **35** 18

pipette [pī pĕt′] **78** 14

pit [pĭt] **8** 37a

pitcher [pĭch′ ər] **29** 4, **93** 12

pitcher's mound [pĭch′ ərz mownd′]
      93 11

pitchfork [pĭch′ förk′] **81** 14

pizza [pēt′ sə] **18** 30

plaid [plăd] **24** 22

plane [plān] **57** 18

planets [plăn′ əts] **74**

plant (v) [plănt] **26** 4

plants (n) [plănts] **60**

plate [plāt] **29** 13

plateau [plă tō′] **88** 1

platform [plăt′ förm′] **54** 11

playground [plā′ grownd′] **87** 15

playpen [plā′ pĕn′] **33** 30

pleasure boating [plĕzh′ ər bō′ tĭng] **59**

pliers [plī′ ərz] **36** 19

plug [plŭg] **37** 43d

plum [plŭm] **9** 34

plumber [plŭm′ ər] **85** 1

plunger [plŭn′ jər] **35** 14

Pluto [ploo′ tō] **74** 19

pocket [pŏk′ ət] **21** 41

pod [pŏd] **6** 17a

podium [pō′ dē əm] **99** 7

poinsettia [poyn sĕt′ ē ə] **60** 15

poison ivy [poy′ zən ī′ vē] **61** 45

poison oak [poy′ zən ōk′] **61** 43

poison sumac [poy′ zən soo′ măk]
      61 44

poisonous plants [poy′ zə nəs plănts′]
      61

polar bear [pōl′ ər bër′] **69** 22

pole [pōl] **94** 34, **95** 14

police officer [pə lēs′ öf′ ə sər] **43** 6

police station [pə lēs′ stā′ shən] **43**

polish [pŏl′ ĭsh] **38** 3

polka dot [pō′ kə dŏt′] **24** 19

pond [pŏnd] **87** 8

pony [pō′ nē] **67** 20

poplar [pŏp′ lər] **61** 30

porch [pörch] **27** 6

porcupine [pör′ kyə pīn′] **66** 11

pork [pörk] **10** 6

pork chops [pörk′ chŏps′] **18** 15

port [pört] **58**

porter [pör′ tər] **56** 5

porthole [pört′ hōl′] **58** 21

post [pōst] **23** 18

post office [pōst′ öf′ ĭs] **44** 9, **46**

postal worker [pōs′ təl wür′ kər] **46** 14

postcard [pōst′ kärd′] **46** 17

postmark [pōst′ märk′] **46** 9

pot [pŏt] **30** 13

pot holder [pŏt′ hōl′ dər] **30** 34

potato chips [pə tā′ tō chĭps′] **18** 4

potato(es) [pə tā′ tō(z)] **7** 23

potty [pŏt′ ē] **33** 33

pouch [powch] **66** 3c

pouched mammals [powcht′ măm′ əlz]
      66

poultry [pōl′ trē] **10**

pour [pör] **31** 4

power lines [pow′ ər līnz′] **80** 24

power sander [pow′ ər săn′ dər] **37** 26

power saw [pow′ ər sö′] **27** 25

power station [pow′ ər stā′ shən] **80** 20

prepositions [prep′ ə zĭ′ shənz]
      102, 103

primates [prī′ māts] **69**

print [prĭnt] **24** 21

printer [prĭn′ tər] **83** 4

printout [prĭnt′ owt′] **83** 8

prints [prĭnts] **100** 11

prism [prĭz′ əm] **78** 1

private jet [prī′ vət jĕt′] **57** 3

produce [prŏd′ oos] **14** 9

programs [prō′ grămz] **99** 17

projector [prə jĕk′ tər] **100** 16

propane gas [prō′ pān găs′] **80** 30

propeller plane [prə pĕl′ ər plān′] **57** 7

prosecuting attorney
      [prŏ′ sə kyoo tĭng ə tür′ nē] **43** 17

prune [proon] **9** 22

public library [pŭb′ lĭk lī′ brër ē] **47**

public transportation
      [pŭb′ lĭk trăns pər tā′ shən] **54**

public telephone [pŭb′ lĭk tĕl′ ə fōn]
      44 7

puck [pŭk] **92** 17

pump [pŭmp] **13** 14, **52** 21

pumpkin [pŭmp′ kĭn] **7** 26

punishment [pŭn′ ĭsh mənt] **43**

pupil [pyoo′ pəl] **5** 48

puppy [pŭp′ ē] **69** 27

purse [pürs] **20** 23

push [poosh] **26** 12

putter [pŭt′ ər] **94** 9

puzzle [pŭz′ əl] **33** 31

pyramid [pïr′ ə mĭd′] **79** 25

quantities [kwŏn′ tə tēz] **12**

quarter [kwör′ tər] **11** 18, **13** 30,
      79 31

quarterback [kwör′ tər băk′] **93** 32

quill [kwĭl] **66** 11a

quilting [kwĭl′ tĭng] **101** 32

rabbit [răb′ ĭt] **66** 13

raccoon [ră koon′] **68** 7

race track [rās′ trăk′] **95**

(racing) handlebars
      [rā′ sĭng hăn′ dəl bärz] **52** 2

rack [răk] **47** 17, **78** 8

racket [răk′ ĭt] **94** 2

racquet [răk′ ĭt] **94** 29

racquetball [răk′ ĭt böl′] **94** 30

radiator [rā′ dē āt′ ər] **51** 56

radio [rā′ dē ō′] **50** 18

radish(es) [răd′ ĭsh (əz)] **7** 29

radius [rā′ dē əs] **79** 14

raft [răft] **89** 16

rafters [răf′ tərz] **82** 1

rafting [răf′ tĭng] **89**

rags [răgz] **35** 4

rain boots [rān′ boots′] **19** 25

raincoat [rān′ kōt′] **21** 38

rainy [rān′ ē] **25** 1

raise (one's hand) [rāz′ wŭnz hănd′]
      77 1

raisin(s) [rā′ zən(z)] **9** 24

rake (v) [rāk] **26** 10

rake (n) [rāk] **27** 30

ranch [rănch] **81**

ranch house [rănch′ hows′] **27**

ranching [rănch′ ĭng] **81**

rapids [răp′ ĭdz] **89** 17

rash [răsh] **40** 1

raspberries [răz′ bĕr′ ēz] **8** 16

rat [răt] **66** 7

rattle [răt′ əl] **33** 21

rattlesnake [răt′ əl snāk′] **65** 10

razor [rā′ zər] **23** 20

razor blades [rā′ zər blādz′] **23** 23

read [rēd] **77** 4

real estate agent [rēl′ ə stāt ā′ jənt]
    85 5

rear bumper [rïr′ bŭm′ pər] **50** 42

rearview mirror [rïr′ vyōō mïr′ ər]
    50 7

receipt [rə sēt′] **15** 20, **55** 24

receiver [rə sē′ vər] **100** 21

receptionist [rə sĕp′ shə nəst] **86** 17

recliner [rə klī′ nər] **28** 16

records [rĕk′ ərdz] **100** 23

rectangle [rĕk′ tăng′ gəl] **79** 19

Red Sea [rĕd′ sē′] **70** 29

redwood [rĕd′ wŏŏd′] **61** 25

(reel of) film [rēl′ əv fĭlm′] **100** 17

referee [rĕf′ ə rē′] **93** 22, **94** 16

reference section
    [rĕf′ ə rəns sĕk′ shən] **47** 21

(reference) librarian
    [rĕf′ ə rəns lī brĕr′ e ən] **47** 23

refill [rē′ fĭl′] **35** 11

refinery [rə fī′ nə rē] **80** 12

reflector [rə flĕk′ tər] **52** 25

refreshment stand
    [rə frĕsh′ mənt stănd′] **90** 2

refrigerator [rə frĭj′ ə rā′ tər] **30** 19

reins [rānz] **94** 22

relationshops [rə lā′ shən shĭps′] **2**

remedies [rĕm′ ə dēz] **41**

remote control [rə mōt′ kən trōl′]
    28 17

repair [rə pĕr′] **38** 10

repairperson [rə pĕr′ pür′ sən] **84** 5

reporter [rə pör′ tər] **86** 11

reptiles [rĕp′ tīlz] **65**

rescue [rĕs′ kyōō] **42**

restaurant [rĕs′ tə rənt] **16**

retriever [rə trē′ vər] **69** 26

return address [rə türn′ ă drĕs′] **46** 8

rhinoceros [rī nŏs′ ə rəs] **66** 16

Rhode Island [rōd′ ī′ lənd] **73** 39

rice [rīs] **60** 21

ride [rīd] **97** 13

rider [rī′ dər] **54** 6

rifle [rī′ fəl] **48** 21

right angle [rīt′ ăng′ gəl] **79** 23

right fielder [rīt′ fēl′ dər] **93** 3

right guard [rīt′ gärd′] **93** 28

right lane [rīt′ lān′] **53** 7

right tackle [rīt′ tăk′ əl] **93** 29

right triangle [rīt′ trī′ ăng gəl] **79** 22

rind [rīnd] **8** 8b

ring(s) [rĭng(z)] **23** 2, **74** 16a, **94** 17

ring binder [rĭng′ bīn′ dər] **76** 14

ring finger [rĭng′ fĭng′ gər] **4** 27

ring stand [rĭng′ stănd′] **78** 19

rink [rĭngk] **94** 25

Rio Grande River [rē′ ō grănd′ rĭv′ ər]
    71 57

rivers [riv′ ərz] **71**

road sign [rōd′ sīn′] **53** 23

road work [rōd′ würk′] **82**

roadrunner [rōd′ rŭn′ ər] **64** 32

roast [rōst] **10** 3, **10** 8

roasting pan [rōs′ tĭng păn′] **30** 17

robes [rōbz] **43** 11

robin [rŏb′ in] **64** 9

rock group [rŏk′ grōōp′] **99**

rocket [rŏk′ ət] **75** 13

rocks [rŏks] **88** 11

rocking chair [rŏk′ ĭng chĕr′] **33** 16

Rocky Mountains [rŏk′ ē mown′ tənz]
    71 40

rodents [rō′ dənts] **66**

roll [rōl] **12** 11, **18** 19

(roll of) film [rōl′ əv fĭlm′] **100** 10

roller [rōl′ ər] **37** 29

rolling pin [rōl′ ĭng pĭn′] **30** 25

rolodex [rōl′ ə dĕks′] **83** 14

rooster [rōō′ stər] **64** 21

roof [rōōf] **27** 4

root [rōōt] **60** 35d

rope [rōp] **89** 23

rose [rōz] **60** 18

rotor [rō′ tər] **57** 2a

rough [rŭf] **95** 6

router [row′ tər] **37** 37

row [rō] **47** 11, **81** 18

rowboat [rō′ bōt′] **59** 23

Rub′ al Khali Desert
    [rōōb′ ăl kŏl′ ē dĕz′ ərt] **71** 52

rubber tubing [rŭb′ ər tōōb′ ĭng] **78** 18

rudder [rŭd′ ər] **59** 5

rug [rŭg] **32** 28

ruler [rōō′ lər] **76** 23

run [rŭn] **96** 6

rung [rŭng] **82** 9

runner [rŭn′ ər] **91** 23, **94** 31

runway [rŭn′ wā′] **57** 19

saddle [săd′ əl] **94** 20

safety glasses [săf′ tē glăs′ əz] **78** 12

safety goggles [săf′ tē gŏg′ əlz] **94** 28

safety pin [săf′ tē pĭn′] **33** 11

Sahara Desert [sə hĕr′ ə dĕz′ ərt]
    71 51

sail [sāl] **59** 9

sailboard [sāl′ börd′] **59** 15

sailboat [sāl′ bōt′] **59** 4

sailor [sāl′ ər] **48** 14

salad bowl [săl′ əd bōl′] **29** 25

salad dressing [săl′ əd drĕs′ ĭng] **18** 12

salamander [săl′ ə măn′ dər] **65** 14

salesperson [sālz′ pür′ sən] **86** 12

salt shaker [sölt′ shā′ kər] **29** 10

sand (v) [sănd] **26** 14

sand (n) [sănd] **90** 31

sand dunes [sănd′ dōōnz′] **90** 12

sand trap [sănd′ trăp′] **95** 11

sandal [săn′ dəl] **20** 19

sandbox [sănd′ bŏks′] **87** 13

sandcastle [sănd′ kăs′ əl] **91** 32

sandpaper [sănd′ pā′ pər] **37** 27

sandwich [sănd′ wĭch] **16** 16

sanitation worker
    [săn ə tā′ shən wür′ kər] **49** 7

Saturn [săt′ ərn] **74** 16

saucepan [sös′ păn′] **30** 8

saucer [sö′ sər] **29** 21

sausage [sö′ sĭj] **10** 7

saw [sö] **36** 8

saxophone [săk′ sə fōn′] **98** 24

scaffolding [skăf′ əl dĭng] **82** 7

scale [skāl] **14** 7, **34** 32, **78** 4

scallop(s) [skăl′ əp(s)] **11** 35, **62** 10

scarecrow [skër′krō′] **81** 19

scarf [skärf] **19** 19

scenery [sē′nə rē] **99** 2

school [skōol] **76, 77**

science lab [sī′əns lăb′] **78**

scissors [sĭz′ərz] **101** 17

scoreboard [skör′börd′] **93** 19

scorpion [skör′pē ən] **63** 8

scouring pad [skowr′ ĭng păd′] **30** 11

scrape [skrāp] **26** 15

scraper [skrāp′ər] **36** 14

screen [skrēn] **27** 19, **100** 14

screw [skrōo] **37** 42

screwdriver [skrōo′drī′vər] **37** 24

scrub [skrŭb] **38** 2

scuba tank [skōo′bə tăngk′] **91** 37

sea gull [sē′gŭl′] **64** 4

sea horse [sē′hörs′] **65** 1

Sea of Japan [sē′əv jə păn′] **70** 36

Sea of Okhotsk [sē′əv ō kŏtsk′]
  70 35

seafood [sē′fōod′] **10**

seal [sēl] **68** 12

seam [sēm] **101** 10

seas [sēz] **70**

seat [sēt] **52** 16, **54** 2

seat belt [sēt′bĕlt′] **50** 23

second baseman [sĕk′ənd bās′mən]
  93 7

secretary [sĕk′rə tër′ē] **83** 11

section [sĕk′shən] **8** 8a, **79** 15

security [sə kyŏor′ə tē] **56**

security guard [sə kyŏor′ə tē gärd′]
  56 9, **86** 14

sedan [sə dăn′] **51**

seed [sēd] **8** 8c

seesaw [sē′sö′] **87** 18

serve [sürv] **17** 3, **96** 2

service area [sür′vəs ër′ē ə] **53** 11

sevice court [sür′vəs kört′] **95** 1

service line [sür′vəs līn′] **95** 3

set (the table) [sĕt′dhə tā′bəl] **17** 8

sewing [sō′ ĭng] **101**

sewing machine [sō′ ĭng mə shēn′]
  101 1

shade [shād] **33** 1

shaft [shăft] **80** 10

shampoo [shăm pōo′] **34** 8

shank [shăngk] **36** 43b

shark [shärk] **65** 5

shaving cream [shā′ vĭng krēm′] **23** 22

sheep [shēp] **67** 25, **81** 10

sheet [shēt] **32** 19

sheet music [shēt′myōo′ zĭk] **98** 2

shelf [shĕlf] **14** 6, **47** 26

shell [shĕl] **48** 27, **62** 1a, **65** 18a,
  90 40

shellfish [shĕl′fĭsh′] **11**

shepherd [shĕp′ərd] **69** 28

shingle [shĭng′gəl] **82** 2

ship [shĭp] **58** 9

shirt [shürt] **21** 46

shock absorbers [shŏk′əb zör′bərz]
  52 31

shoe [shōo] **21** 49

shoelace [shōo′lās′] **20** 7

shoot [shōot] **97** 16

shop worker [shŏp′wür′kər] **85** 12

shopping bag [shŏp′ ĭng băg′] **20** 18

shopping basket [shŏp′ ĭng băs′kət]
  14 8

shopping cart [shŏp′ ĭng kärt′] **15** 19

short [shört] **24** 1

short sleeve [shört′slēv′] **20** 21

shorts [shörts] **20** 14

shortstop [shört′stŏp′] **93** 5

shoulder [shōl′dər] **4** 5, **53** 22

(shoulder) bag [shōl′dər băg′] **21** 35

shovel (n) [shŭv′əl] **27** 31, **82** 15,
  90 17

shovel (v) [shŭv′əl] **26** 13

shower cap [show′ər kăp′] **34** 3

shower curtain [show′ər kür′tən] **34** 5

shower head [show′ər hĕd′] **34** 4

shrimp [shrĭmp] **11** 31, **62** 8

shutter [shŭt′ər] **27** 8

shuttle car [shŭt′əl kär′] **80** 8

side [sīd] **79** 10

side mirror [sīd′mïr′ər] **50** 2

sideburn [sīd′bürn′] **4** 33

sidewalk [sīd′wök′] **45** 25

Sierra Madre [sē ër′ə mö′drē] **71** 42

silo [sī′lō] **81** 4

silverware [sĭl′vər wër′] **29** 22

simple animals [sĭm′pəl ăn′ə məlz] **62**

singer [sĭng′ər] **99** 24

sink [sĭngk] **34** 19

sister [sĭs′tər] **3** 10

sister-in-law [sĭs′tər ən lö′] **3** 8

six-pack [sĭks′păk′] **13** 13

skate (n) [skāt] **94** 26

skate (v) [skāt] **97** 9

skein [skān] **101** 24

ski [skē] **95** 17

ski boot [skē′bōot′] **95** 15

ski cap [skē′kăp′] **19** 16

ski lift [skē′lĭft′] **95** 18

ski slope [skē′slōp′] **95**

skier [skē′ər] **94** 35

skis [skēz] **94** 33

skin [skĭn] **9** 37b

skirt [skürt] **21** 36

skunk [skŭngk] **68** 8

slacks [slăks] **20** 4

sleeping bag [slē′pĭng băg′] **89** 26

sleepwear [slēp′wër′] **22**

slice (n) [slīs] **13** 21

slice (v) [slīs] **31** 10

slide [slīd] **78** 31, **87** 12

slide projector [slīd′prə jĕk′tər]
  100 13

slides [slīdz] **100** 12

sling [slĭng] **39** 3

splippers [slĭp′ərz] **22** 18

slug [slŭg] **62** 4

small [smöl] **24** 7

smoke [smōk] **42** 15

smoke detector [smōk′də tĕk′tər]
  33 15

smokestack [smök′stăk′] **58** 18,
  80 22

snacks [snăks] **14** 18

snail [snāl] **62** 1

snake [snāk] **65** 9

snap [snăp] **101** 13

sneakers [snē′kərz] **20** 11

snorkel [snör′kəl] **91** 34

snow plow [snō′plow′] **49** 5

snowy [snō′e] **25** 3

soap [sōp] **34** 15

soap dish [sōp′dĭsh′] **34** 6

soccer [sŏk′ər] **92**

soccer ball [sŏk′ər böl′] **92** 26

socks [sŏks] **22** 17

sofa [sō**/**fə] **28** 25

soft drink [söft**/** drĭngk**/**] **16** 11

softball [söft**/** böl**/**] **92, 92** 10

solar collector [sō**/** lər kə lĕk**/** tər] **80** 17

solar eclipse [sō**/** lər ĭ klĭps**/**] **74** 10

solar system [sō**/** lər sĭs**/** təm] **74**

soldier [sōl**/** jər] **48** 16

sole [sōl] **20** 6

solid [sŏl**/** əd] **24** 20

solid figures [sŏl**/** əd fĭg**/** yərz] **79**

son [sŭn] **3** 16

Sony Walkman [sō**/** nē wök**/** mən] **100** 30

sore throat [sör**/** thrōt**/**] **40** 12

south [sowth] **71** 72

South America [sowth**/** ə mër**/** ə kə] **70** 2

South Atlantic [sowth**/** ăt lăn**/** tək] **70** 12

South Carolina [sowth**/** kăr ə lī**/** nə] **73** 40

South China Sea [sowth**/** chi**/** nə sē**/**] **70** 39

South Dakota [sowth**/** də kō**/** tə] **73** 41

South Pacific [sowth pə sĭf**/** ək] **70** 10

space probe [spās**/** prōb] **75** 4

space program [spās**/** prō**/** grăm] **75**

space shuttle [spās**/** shŭt**/** əl] **75** 14

space station [spās**/** stā**/** shən] **75** 1

space suit [spās**/** sōōt**/**] **75** 6

spacecraft [spās**/** krăft**/**] **75**

spaghetti [spə gĕt**/** ē] **18** 10

spaniel [spăn**/** yəl] **69** 24

spare ribs [spër**/** rĭbz**/**] **10** 10

spare tire [spër**/** tīr**/**] **51** 39

sparrow [spăr**/** ō] **64** 10

spatula [spăch**/** ə lə] **27** 21

speaker [spē**/** kər] **28** 21, **100** 24

speed limit sign [spēd**/** lĭm ət sīn**/**] **53** 8

speedometer [spə dŏm**/** ə tər] **50** 10

spider [spī**/** dər] **63** 16

spinach [spĭn**/** əch] **6** 8

spinal cord [spī**/** nəl körd**/**] **5** 58

spiral notebook [spī**/** rəl nōt**/** bŏŏk] **76** 15

split [splĭt] **11** 17

split end [splĭt**/** ĕnd**/**] **93** 24

spoke [spōk] **52** 26

sponge [spŭnj] **34** 7

(sponge) mop [spŭnj**/** mŏp**/**] **35** 6

(spool of) thread [spōōl**/** əv thrĕd**/**] **101** 2

spoon [spōōn] **29** 8

sports car [spörts**/** kär**/**] **53** 17

sports [spörts] **92-97**

spotlight [spŏt**/** līt**/**] **99** 4

sprain [sprān] **40** 13

spray can [sprā**/** kăn**/**] **13** 24

spray starch [sprā**/** stärch**/**] **35** 21

spread [sprĕd] **17** 11

Spring [sprĭng] **26**

sprinkler [sprĭng**/** klər] **27** 13, **87** 14

sprocket [sprŏk**/** ət] **52** 20

square [skwër] **79** 9

squid [skwĭd] **62** 5

squirrel [skwür**/** əl] **66** 10

stage [stāj] **99** 5

staircase [stër**/** kās] **28** 12

stake [stāk] **89** 30

stamp [stămp] **46** 10

stands [stăndz] **93** 10

staple remover [stāp**/** əl rə moo**/** vər] **83** 29

stapler [stāp**/** lər] **83** 27

star [stär] **74** 4

starfish [stär**/** fĭsh**/**] **62** 7

starting gate [stär**/** tĭng gāt**/**] **95** 20

station [stā**/** shən] **55** 18

station wagon [stā**/** shən wăg**/** ən] **50**

steak [stāk] **10** 5, **11** 29, **18** 21

steam [stēm] **31** 12

steamer [stēm**/** ər] **30** 3

steering wheel [stür**/** ĭng wēl**/**] **50** 8

stem [stĕm] **8** 2a, **60** 1a

step [stĕp] **28** 13

stepladder [stĕp**/** lăd**/** ər] **35** 1

stereo cassette player [stër**/** ē ō kə sĕt plā**/** ər] **100** 25

stereo system [stër**/** ē ō sĭs**/** təm] **28** 20

stern [stürn] **58** 11

stethoscope [stĕth**/** ə skōp**/**] **39** 9

stewing meat [stoo**/** ĭng mēt] **10** 4

stick [stĭk] **12** 5

stick shift [stĭk**/** shĭft**/**] **50** 24

sting [stĭng] **63** 8a

stingray [stĭng**/** rā**/**] **65** 6

stir [stür] **31** 1

stitch [stĭch] **101** 19

stitches [stĭch**/** əz] **39** 21

stockings [stŏk**/** ĭngz] **22** 6

stomach [stŭm**/** ək] **5** 66

stomachache [stŭm**/** ək āk**/**] **40** 7

stool [stōōl] **78** 34

stopper [stŏp**/** ər] **34** 10, **78** 10

stork [störk] **64** 30

stove [stōv] **30** 30

straight line [strāt**/** līn**/**] **79** 1

(strand of) beads [strănd**/** əv bēdz**/**] **23** 7

strap [străp] **54** 8

straw [strö] **16** 10

strawberry [strö**/** bër**/** ē] **8** 15

strawberry shortcake [strö**/** bër ē shört**/** kāk] **18** 26

stream [strēm] **88** 6

street [strēt] **45** 31

street cleaner [strēt**/** klē**/** nər] **49** 1

street sign [strēt**/** sīn**/**] **44** 8

streetcar [strēt**/** kär**/**] **55** 30

streetlight [strēt**/** līt**/**] **45** 29

stretch [strĕch] **95** 19

stretch bandage [strĕch**/** băn**/** dĭj] **40** 13a

stretcher [strĕch**/** ər] **39** 12

stretchie [strĕch**/** ē] **33** 19

string [strĭng] **46** 20, **98** 10a

string bean(s) [strĭng**/** bēn(z)**/**] **6** 15

strings [strĭngz] **98**

striped [strīpt] **24** 17

stroller [strō**/** lər] **33** 14

student [stōō**/** dənt] **76** 19

stuffed animal [stŭft**/** ăn ə məl] **33** 27

subject [sŭb**/** jəkt] **47** 10

submarine [sŭb**/** mə rēn**/**] **48** 7

subway [sŭb**/** wā**/**] **54**

subway station [sŭb**/** wā stā**/** shən] **44** 16

sugar (packet) [shōōg**/** ər păk**/** ət] **16** 13

sugar bowl [shōōg**/** ər bōl**/**] **29** 23

sugarcane [shōōg**/** ər kān**/**] **60** 20

suitcase [sōōt**/** kās**/**] **56** 7

Summer [sŭm**/** ər] **26**

sun [sŭn] **74** 7, **80** 3

sunbather [sŭn/ bā/ dhər] **90** 19

sundae [sŭn/ dē] **18** 23

sunflower [sŭn/ flŏw/ ər] **60** 19

sunglasses [sŭn/ glăs/ əz] **90** 14

sunny [sŭn/ ē] **25** 4

(sunnyside-up) egg
   [sŭn/ ē sīd ŭp/ ĕg/] **18** 32

sunroof [sŭn/ rōof/] **51** 44

suntan lotion [sŭn/ tăn lō/ shən] **91** 39

supermarket [sōo/ pər mär/ kət] **14**

surf [sürf] **97** 12

surfboard [sürf/ börd/] **91** 25

surgery [sŭr/ jə rē] **41** 2

suspect [sŭs/ pĕkt] **43** 3

swan [swŏn] **64** 28

sweatband [swĕt/ bănd/] **20** 12

sweater [swĕt/ ər] **19** 7, **19** 13, **19** 23

sweatpants [swĕt/ pănts/] **20** 10

sweatshirt [swĕt/ shürt/] **20** 8

sweep [swēp] **38** 7

swimmer [swĭm/ ər] **91** 28

swing [swĭng] **33** 24

swings [swĭngz] **87** 16

switch [swĭch] **37** 43c

switchboard [swĭch/ börd/] **83** 3

switchboard operator
   [swĭch/ börd ŏp/ ə rā tər] **83** 1

swordfish [sörd/ fĭsh/] **65** 3

synthesizer [sĭn/ thə sī/ zər] **99** 21

syringe [sə rĭnj/] **39** 27

syrup [sĭr/ əp] **18** 6

T-shirt [tē/ shürt/] **21** 29

table [tā/ bəl] **29** 7

tablecloth [tā/ bəl klŏth/] **29** 16

tablet [tăb/ lət] **41** 6

taco [tŏ/ kō] **18** 24

tadpole [tăd/ pōl/] **65** 16

tail [tāl] **57** 10, **65** 3a, **66** 3a

taillight [tāl/ līt/] **50** 31

tailor [tā/ lər] **84** 6

take [tāk] **17** 10

takeoff [tāk/ ŏf/] **57**

Takla Makan Desert
   [tŏk/ lə mə kŏn/ dĕz/ ərt] **71** 53

tambourine [tăm/ bə rēn/] **98** 17

tank [tăngk] **48** 10

tank top [tăngk/ tŏp/] **20** 13

tanker [tăngk/ ər] **58** 15

tap [tăp] **16** 20

tape [tāp] **46** 22

tape measure [tāp/ mĕzh/ ər] **36** 21,
   101 15

taxi [tăk/ sē] **55**

taxi stand [tăk/ sē stănd/] **55** 28

taxicab [tăk/ sē kăb/] **55** 27

tea [tē] **16** 15

teacher [tē/ chər] **76** 4

teakettle [tē/ kĕt/ əl] **30** 28

team sports [tēm/ spörts/] **92**

teapot [tē/ pŏt/] **29** 19

tear [tër] **77** 9

teddy bear [tĕd/ ē bër/] **33** 3

tee [tē] **95** 13

telephone [tĕl/ ə fōn/] **83** 15

telescope [tĕl/ ə skōp/] **74** 22

television [tĕl/ ə vĭzh/ ən] **28** 18, **100** 5

teller [tĕl/ ər] **86** 15

temperature [tĕm/ pər ə chər] **25** 6

Tennessee [tĕn/ ə sē/] **73** 42

tennis [tĕn/ əs] **94**

tennis ball [tĕn/ əs böl/] **94** 1

tennis court [tĕn/ əs kört/] **95**

tent [tĕnt] **89** 24

tentacle [tĕn/ tə kəl] **62** 12a

terminal [türm/ ə nəl] **51** 55, **58** 29

terminal building [türm/ ə nəl bĭl/ dĭng]
   57 16

termite [tür/ mīt] **63** 11

terrier [tĕr/ ē ər] **69** 25

test tube [tĕst/ tōob/] **78** 9

Texas [tĕk/ səs] **73** 43

textbook [tĕkst/ bŏok/] **76** 26

theater [thē/ ə tər] **99**

thermometer
   [thər möm/ ə tər] **25** 5, **78** 22

thermos [thür/ məs] **88** 14

thigh [thī] **4** 18, **11** 19

thimble [thĭm/ bəl] **101** 21

third (1/3) [thürd] **79** 32

third baseman [thürd/ bās/ mən] **93** 4

thorn [thörn] **60** 18c

thread [thrĕd] **37** 42b, **101** 2

three-piece suit [thrē/ pēs sōot] **21** 40

throat [thrōt] **5** 59

through [thrōo] **103** 1

throw [thrō] **97** 10

thumb [thŭm] **4** 24

thumbtack [thŭm/ tăk/] **76** 25

ticket [tĭk/ ət] **55** 16, **56** 4

ticket window [tĭk/ ət wĭn/ dō] **55** 19

tie (n) [tī] **21** 47

tie (v) [tī] **77** 12

tie clip [tī/ klĭp/] **23** 14

tie pin [tī/ pĭn/] **23** 13

tiger [tī/ gər] **68** 2

tight [tīt] **24** 3

tighten [tī/ tən] **38** 4

tight end [tīt/ ĕnd/] **93** 30

tights [tīts] **19** 14

tile [tīl] **34** 27

timer [tī/ mər] **78** 13

timetable [tīm/ tă/ bəl] **55** 20

tip [tĭp] **55** 22

tire [tīr] **50** 37, **52** 28

tissues [tĭsh/ ōoz] **32** 13

title [tī/ təl] **47** 9

to [tōo] **103** 9

toast [tōst] **18** 34

toaster [tōs/ tər] **30** 16

toe [tō] **5** 54

toenail [tō/ nāl/] **5** 56

toilet [toy/ lət] **34** 29

toilet brush [toy/ lət brŭsh/] **34** 31

toilet paper [toy/ lət pā/ pər] **34** 30

toiletries [toy/ lə trēz] **23**

token booth [tō/ kən bōoth/] **54** 13

tollbooth [tōl/ bōoth/] **53** 27

tomato(es) [tə mā/ tō(z)] **6** 19

tongs [tŏngz] **78** 29

tongue [tŭng] **4** 41

tongue depressor [tŭng/ də prĕs/ ər]
   40 12a

toolbox [tōol/ bŏks/] **36** 23

toolshed [tōol/ shĕd/] **27** 28

tooth [tōoth] **4** 42

toothache [tōoth/ āk/] **40** 9

toothbrush [tōoth/ brŭsh/] **34** 21

toothless mammals [tōoth/ ləs măm/ əlz]
   66

toothpaste [tōoth/ pāst/] **34** 16

tortoise [tör/ təs] **65** 18

tossed salad [tōst/ săl/ əd] **18** 13

touch [tŭch] **77** 2

touring handlebars
    [tŏŏr' ĭng hăn' dəl bärz] **52** 12
tow truck [tō' trŭk] **49** 2
toward [törd] **103** 4
towel rack [tow' əl răk'] **34** 25
towrope [tō' rōp'] **59** 11
toy chest [toy' chĕst'] **33** 29
track [trăk] **54** 10, **94** 32
track and field [trăk' ənd fēld'] **94**
tractor [trăk' tər] **81** 15
tractor trailer [trăk' tər trā' lər] **49** 15
traffic cop [trăf' ək kŏp'] **44** 10
traffic light [trăf' ək līt'] **45** 21
trailer [trā' lər] **53** 10
train [trān] **55**
training wheels [trān' ĭng wēlz'] **52** 1
transcript [trăn' skrĭpt] **43** 15
transfer [trăns' fər] **54** 4
transformer [trăns för' mər] **80** 25
transmission towers
    [trănz mĭsh' ən tow' ərz] **80** 23
transportation [trăns' pər tā' shən] **54**
transporter [trăns' pör tər] **49** 17
trash basket [trăsh' băs' kət] **44** 15
trash can [trăsh' kăn'] **87** 11
travel agent [trăv' əl ā' jənt] **84** 4
traveler [trăv' ə lər] **56** 3
tray [trā] **16** 33
tray table [trā' tā' bəl] **56** 22
treatments [trēt' mənts] **41**
tree [trē] **61** 35
trees [trēz] **60**
triangle [trī' ăng' gəl] **79** 6
tricycle [trī' sĭ kəl] **52** 6
trigger [trĭg' ər] **48** 22
tripod [trī' pod] **100** 9
trim [trĭm] **26** 8
trombone [trŏm bōn'] **98** 23
trough [tröf] **81** 25
trout [trowt] **65** 2
trowel [trow' əl] **27** 27
truck [trŭk] **49**, **53** 25
truck driver [trŭk' drī' vər] **49** 16
trumpet [trŭm' pət] **98** 25
trunk [trŭngk] **51** 40, **61** 35b, **66** 17a
tub [tŭb] **12** 6
tuba [tōō' bə] **98** 27
tube [tōōb] **13** 15, **91** 29

tugboat [tŭg' bōt'] **58** 13
tulip [tōō' ləp] **60** 1
turkey [tür' kē] **10** 23, **64** 20
turnip [tür' nəp] **6** 34
turn signal lever [türn' sĭg nəl lĕ' vər]
    50 11
turn signal lights [türn' sĭg nəl līts']
    51 50
turnstile [türn' stīl'] **54** 12
turntable [türn' tā' bəl] **100** 18
turtle [tür' təl] **65** 12
(turtleneck) sweater
    [tür' təl nĕk swĕ' tər] **19** 13
tusk [tŭsk] **66** 17b
TV antenna [tē' vē ăn tĕn' ə] **27** 3
tweezers [twē' zərz] **78** 32
twig [twĭg] **61** 33a
(two-door) sedan [tōō' dör sə dăn'] **51**
type [tīp] **77** 10
typewriter [tīp' rī' tər] **83** 10
typing chair [tī' pĭng chër'] **83** 17
typist [tī' pəst] **83** 6
U.S. mailbox [yōō' ĕs māl' bŏks] **46** 6
U.S. Postal System
    [yōō' ĕs pōs' təl sĭs təm] **46**
ukulele [yōō' kə lā' lē] **98** 3
umbrella [ŭm brĕl' ə] **20** 24
umpire [ŭm' pīr] **92** 1, **93** 17
uncle [ŭng' kəl] **3** 3
under [ŭn' dər] **102** 8
underpants [ŭn' dər pănts'] **22** 3
undershirt [ŭn' dər shürt'] **22** 1
underwear [ŭn' dər wër'] **22**
uniform [yōō' nə förm'] **21** 45, **92** 9
United States of America
    [yōō nī' təd stāts' əv əmër' ə kə] **72**
universe [yōō' nə vürs'] **74**
up [ŭp] **103** 11
upper arm [ŭp' ər ärm'] **4** 7
Urals [yŏŏr' əlz] **71** 46
uranium rods [yŏŏ rā' nē əm rŏdz']
    80 15
Uranus [yŏŏr' ə nəs] **74** 17
usher [ŭsh' ər] **99** 16
Utah [yōō' tö] **73** 44
utility pole [yōō tĭl' ə tē pōl'] **80** 26
utility room [yōō tĭl' ə tē rōōm'] **35**

(V-neck) sweater [vē' nĕk swĕt' ər]
    19 23
vacuum [văk' yōōm] **38** 14
vacuum cleaner [văk' yōōm klē' nər]
    35 16
valve [vălv] **52** 27
van [văn] **53** 26
vase [vās] **28** 6
VCR (videocassette recorder)
    [vē' sē är']/
    [vĭd' ē ō kə sĕt' rə kör' dər] **100** 4
vegetables [vĕj' tə bəlz] **6**
vehicles and equipment
    [vē' ə kəlz ənd ə kwĭp' mənt] **48**
vein [vān] **5** 68
vendor [vĕn' dər] **87** 3
vent [vĕnt] **50** 21
Venus [vē' nəs] **74** 12
verbs [vürbz] **17**, **26**, **31**, **38**, **77**, **96**
Vermont [vür mŏnt'] **73** 45
vest [vĕst] **21** 39
video [vĭd' ē ō] **100**
video camera [vĭd' ē ō kăm' ə rə]
    100 1
videocassette (tape)
    [vĭd' ē ō kə sĕt' tāp'] **100** 3
vine [vīn] **61** 42
viola [vē ōl' ə] **98** 8
violet [vī' ə lət] **60** 16
violin [vī ə lĭn'] **98** 7
Virginia [vər jĭn' yə] **73** 46
vise [vīs] **37** 36
visor [vīz' ər] **50** 5
volleyball [vŏl' ē böl'] **92**, **92** 22
waders [wā' dərz] **88** 10
waist [wāst] **4** 13
waiter [wā tər] **16** 5
waitress [wā' trəs] **16** 2
walk [wök] **77** 8
walker [wök' ər] **33** 23
wall [wöl] **28** 3
wall unit [wöl' yōō' nət] **28** 19
wall-to-wall carpeting
    [wöl' tə wöl kär' pə tĭng] **28** 15
wallet [wöl' ət] **20** 9
walnut(s) [wöl' nət(s)] **8** 29
walrus [wöl' rŭs] **68** 11
warm [wörm] **25** 8

wash [wŏsh] **38** 16

washcloth [wŏsh′klöth′] **34** 22

washer [wŏsh′ ər] **37** 40

washing machine
[wŏsh′ ĭng mə shēn′] **35** 30

Washington [wŏsh′ ĭng tən] **73** 47

wasp [wŏsp] **63** 20

wastepaper basket
[wāst′ pā pər băs′ kət] **34** 13

watch [wŏch] **23** 10

watchband [wŏch′ bănd′] **23** 11

water (*n*) [wŏt′ ər] **42** 16, **91** 30

water (*v*) [wŏt′ ər] **26** 5

water fountain [wŏt′ ər fown′ tən]
87 19

water glass [wŏt′ ər glăs′] **29** 6

waterfall [wŏt′ər föl] **80** 11, **89** 18

water-skier [wŏt′ər skē′ ər] **59** 10

watercress [wŏt′ər krĕs′] **6** 5

watering can [wŏt′ər ĭng kăn′] **27** 16

watermelon [wŏt′ər mĕl′ ən] **9** 26

wave [wāv] **91** 24

weapon [wĕp′ənz] **48**

weather [wĕdh′ər] **25**

weather forecaster
[wĕdh′ ər för′ kăst ər] **86** 1

weather satellite [wĕdh′ər săt′ ə līt]
75 3

weaving [wē′ vĭng] **101** 30

web [wĕb] **63** 15

wedding ring [wĕd′ ĭng rĭng′] **23** 4

weights [wāts] **78** 5

west [wĕst] **71** 74

West Virginia [wĕst′ vər jĭn′ yə] **73** 48

wet [wĕt] **25** 15

wet suit [wĕt′ sōot′] **91** 38

whale [wāl] **68** 9

wheat [wēt] **60** 22

wheat farm [wēt′ färm′] **81**

(wheat) field [wēt′ fēld′] **81** 16

wheel [wēl] **52** 4

wheelbarrow [wēl′ băr′ ō] **27** 32,
82 23

wheelchair [wēl′ chër′] **39** 2

whistle [wĭs′ əl] **90** 5

whole [hōl] **11** 27, **79** 29

whole (chicken) [hōl′ chĭk′ ən] **11** 16

width [wĭdth] **79** 35

wife [wīf] **2** 4

willow [wĭl′ ō] **61** 31

wind [wĭnd] **80** 4

windbreaker [wĭnd′ brā′ kər] **19** 5

windlass [wĭnd′ ləs] **58** 23

windmill [wĭnd′ mĭl′] **80** 19

window [wĭn′ dō] **27** 7, **46** 15

window cleaner [wĭn′ dō klē′ nər]
35 10

windpipe [wĭnd′ pīp′] **5** 60

windshield [wĭnd′ shēld′] **51** 45

windshield wiper [wĭnd′ shēld wī′ pər]
50 6

windsurfer [wĭnd′ sür′ fər] **59** 14

windy [wĭn′ dē] **25** 13

wine [wīn] **16** 19

wine glass [wīn′ glăs′] **29** 5

wing [wĭng] **11** 22, **57** 9, **63** 4a,
64 1a

Winter [wĭn′ tər] **26**

wipe [wīp] **38** 5

wire [wīr] **37** 35

wire mesh screen [wīr′ mĕsh skrēn′]
78 6

Wisconsin [wĭs kŏn′ sən] **73** 49

witness [wĭt′ nəs] **43** 13

witness stand [wĭt′ nəs stănd′] **43** 18

wolf [wŏolf] **69** 29

woman [wŏom′ən] **2** 1

wood [wŏod] **36** 4

wood plane [wŏod′ plān′] **37** 32

woodpecker [wŏod′ pĕk′ ər] **64** 17

woods [wŏodz] **89** 32

woodwinds [wŏod′ wĭndz′] **98**

wool [wŏol] **101** 23

word processor [würd′ prŏ′ sĕs ər]
83 7

work gloves [würk′ glŭvz′] **27** 26

workbench [würk′ bĕnch′] **36** 22

workshop [würk′ shŏp′] **36**

world [würld] **70**

worm [würm] **62** 11

wrench [rĕnch] **36** 10

wrist [rĭst] **4** 21

write [rīt] **77** 7

writer [rī′ tər] **86** 7

Wyoming [wī ō′ mĭng] **73** 50

X ray [ĕks′ rā′] **39** 1

X ray screener [ĕks′ rā skrē′ nər] **56** 11

xylophone [zī′ lə fōn′] **98** 31

yam [yăm] **7** 24

Yangtze River [yăng′ sē rĭv′ ər] **71** 69

yarn [yärn] **101** 31

Yellow Sea [yĕl′ ō sē′] **70** 37

Yenisey River [yĕn′ ə sā′ rĭv′ ər]
71 65

Yukon River [yōo′ kŏn rĭv′ ər] **71** 56

zebra [zē′ brə] **66** 18

zinnia [zĭn′ ē ə] **60** 13

zip code [zĭp′ kōd′] **46** 12

zipper [zĭp′ ər] **101** 16

zoo [zōo] **87** 1

zucchini [zōo kē′ nē] **7** 27

abażur **28** 27

adapter **100** 18

adres **46** 11

adres zwrotny **46** 8

adwokat **43** 22

Afryka **70** 4

agent policji **43** 2

agrafka **33** 11

agrest **8** 11

akordeon **98** 28

aksamitka **60** 6

aktor **99** 19

aktorka **99** 20

aktówka **21** 37

akumulator **51** 54

Alabama **72** 1

Alaska **72** 2

alejka dla biegaczy **87** 9

aligator **65** 8

Alpy **71** 44

altówka **98** 8

Amazonka **71** 59

Ameryka Południowa **70** 2

Ameryka Północna **70** 1

amortyzatory **52** 31

ananas **8** 4

Andy **71** 43

Antarktyda **70** 7

antena **51** 46

antena telewizyjna **27** 3

antresola **99** 13

aparat **100** 8

Appalachy **71** 41

apteczka **34** 14

apteka **45** 22

aptekarz **84** 1

arbuz **9** 26

architekt **85** 8

archiwista **83** 23

areszt **43** 1

Arizona **72** 3

Arkansas **72** 4

artysta plastyk **86** 3

asteroida **74** 20

astronauta **75** 5

atlas **47** 20

Australia **70** 6

autobus **53** 20, **54**

automat telefoniczny **44** 7

autor **47** 8, **86** 7

autostopowicz **53** 9

autostrada międzystanowa **53** 1

Azja **70** 5

awokado **9** 33

babcia **3** 1

bagaż **56** 8

bagaż podręczny **56** 2

bagażnik **51** 40

bagażowy **56** 5

bagnet **48** 24, **51** 58

bak **4** 33

bakłażan **7** 21

balet **99**

balkon **99** 14

balon na ciepłe powietrze **57** 1

bandaż (gazowy) **39** 24

bandaż elastyczny **40** 13a

banjo **98** 5

banknoty dolarowe **13** 25

bankowość **86**

bar **16** 24

bar koktailowy **16**

baranina **10** 13

bariera (środkowa) **53** 18, **82** 24

bark **4** 5

barka **58** 12

barman **16** 21

baseball **92**

baseball—mała liga **92**

Basen Antarktyczny **70** 14

batuta **99** 9

baza **93** 6

baza-meta **93** 15

bażant **64** 19

bączek **59** 18

befsztyk **10** 5, **18** 21

bekon **18** 33

benzyna **80** 28

beret **19** 22

betoniarka **82** 25

bezpiecznik **35** 5

bęben **98** 19

biblioteczka **28** 22

biblioteka publiczna **47**

bibliotekarka **47** 1

bibliotekarka (działu
  podręcznego) **47** 23

biec **96** 6

biedronka **63** 14

biegacz **94** 31

biegacze **91** 23

bielinka **35** 26

bielizna do prania **35** 28

bielizna dzienna i nocna **22**

bieżnia **94** 32

bilet **55** 16, **56** 4

bilet na przesiadkę **54** 4

bileter **99** 16

biodro **4** 16

biurko **28** 14, **83** 13

biuro podróży **84** 4

biuro **83**

biurowiec **44** 1

bizon **67** 19

biżuteria **23**

blacha do pieczenia **30** 17

blat **30** 27

blezer **21** 26

blok do pisania (pism
  prawniczych) **83** 26

blokada drzwi **50** 1

bluszcz jadowity **61** 45

bluza **19** 17

bluza od dresu **20** 8

bluzka **21** 34

błotnik **52** 10

bochenek **12** 7

bocian **64** 30

boczek **10** 11, **18** 33

boiska do gry w piłkę **93**

boiska i tereny sportowe **95**

boja **58** 16

bok **79** 10

boks **94**

bóbr **66** 12

ból brzucha **40** 7

ból gardła **40** 12

ból głowy **40** 6

ból pleców **40** 8

ból zęba **40** 9

bom **59** 7

bomba **48** 3

bombowiec **48** 2

bongosy **98** 22

bor **39** 15

bowling **94**

brać **17** 10

bramka **92** 25

bramkarz **92** 24

bransoleta **23** 9

brat **3** 9

bratek **60** 2

brew **5** 44

broda **4** 39

brokuły **6** 2

broń i amunicja **48**

brudny **24** 5

brukselka **6** 4

brygadzista **85** 13

bryły **79**

brzoskwinia **9** 37

brzoza **61** 32

brzuch **4** 14

budownictwo **82**

budowniczy **82** 5

budynek dworca lotniczego **57** 16

budzik **32** 8

bufet **90** 2

bujak **33** 16

bulaj **58** 21

bułka **18** 7

burak **7** 33

but **21** 49

but narciarski **95** 15

butelka **12** 3, **33** 17

butla z powietrzem **91** 37

buty robocze **21** 32

buty sportowe **20** 11

bydło (w stadzie) **81** 20

byk **67** 34

bystrza **89** 17

calówka **36** 1

cała **11** 27

całość **79** 29

cążki do paznokci **23** 31

cebula **7** 31

cebulka **60** 8a

cedzak **30** 7

cegły **82** 12

celownik **95** 21

cement **82** 10

cent **13** 27

chleb **14** 12

chłodnica **51** 56

chłodno **25** 9

chłopiec **2** 8

chłopiec podający pałki **93** 18

chodnik **45** 25

chodnik z desek **90** 1

chodzik **33** 23

chór **99** 18

chorągiewka **82** 20

chrupki ziemniaczane **18** 4

chryzantema **60** 4

chrząszcz **63** 10

chusteczki **33** 8

chusteczki papierowe **32** 13

ciało **4**

ciało człowieka **4–5**

ciąć **31** 9

ciąć w plasterki **31** 10

ciągnik siodłowy **49** 15

ciasny **24** 3

ciastka **18** 22

cielę **67** 31

ciemny **24** 10

cień do powiek **23** 30

ciepła bielizna **22** 7

ciepło **25** 8, **80** 27

cierń **60** 18c

ciężarówka **53** 25

ciężarówki **49**

ciotka **3** 6

Connecticut **72** 7

córka **3** 15

cukier (w torebce) **16** 13

cukiernica **29** 23

cukinia **7** 27

cuma **58** 25

cykada **63** 5

cykoria **6** 7

cynia **60** 13

cysterna z paliwem **49** 3

cytryna **8** 9

czajnik **30** 28

czapka **19** 2, **21** 43, **92** 11

czapka narciarska **19** 16

czarna jagoda **8** 14

cząstka **8** 8a

czek **15** 27

czepek kąpielowy **34** 3

część koła **79** 15

czołg **48** 10

czoło **4** 32

czosnek **7** 25

czterodrzwiowy z tylną klapą **51**

czujnik rentgenowski **56** 11

czułek **62** 12a

czynele **98** 18

czyścić **26** 2

czysty **24** 6

czytać **77** 4

czytnik mikrofilmów **47** 14

ćwiartka **11** 18, **79** 31

dach **27** 4

dachówka **82** 2

Dakota Południowa **73** 41

Dakota Północna **73** 34

daktyl **9** 23

daszek **50** 5

dąb **61** 33

dąb jadowity **61** 43

deck kasetowy **100** 22

dekiel **50** 36

dekoracje **99** 2

Delaware **72** 8

delfin **68** 13

dentysta **39** 17

dereń **61** 28

deska **30** 26, **59** 15, **82** 16

deska do prasowania **35** 13

deska rozdzielcza **50** 19

deska surfingowa **91** 25

deska treningowa **91** 27

deszczowa **25** 1

dętka **91** 29

diament baseballowy **93**

disc jockey **86** 9

dłoń **4** 29

długi **24** 2

długi rękaw **20** 15

długie buty **19** 21

długopis **76** 22

długość **79** 36

do **103** 12

dojeżdżający **55** 17

dok **58** 28

dokręcać **38** 4

dolegliwości **40**

dołek **94** 8

dom dla lalek **33** 25

dom na farmie **27**

dom mieszkalny **45** 23, **81** 3

dom towarowy **44** 5

dom w stylu kolonialnym **27**

donica do mieszania **30** 24

doręczanie poczty **46**

doręczyciel **46** 3

dostawca **85** 10

dotknąć **77** 2

dozorca **85** 9

dozownik **13** 14

drabina **35** 1, **42** 1, **82** 8

drążek na zasłonę **34** 1

dreszcze **40** 4

drewniane instrumenty dęte **98**

drewno **36** 4

drozd wędrowny **64** 9

drób **11**

drugi pilot **56** 16

drukarka **83** 4

drut **37** 35, **101** 25

drzewa **61**

drzewo **61** 35

drzewo owocowe **81** 2

drzwi ładowni **57** 13

dudek **64** 32

dulka **59** 21

duży **24** 8

duży palec **5** 53

dwadzieścia pięć centów **13** 30

dworzec **58** 29

dym **42** 15

dynia **7** 26

dyrygent **99** 8

dystans **95** 19

dystrybutor **53** 14

Dystrykt Kolumbii **73** 51

dysza **42** 17

dywan **28** 15, **32** 28

dywanik **50** 22

dzbanek **29** 4

dzbanek do kawy **29** 18

dzbanek do robienia kawy **30** 31

dzbanek na herbatę **29** 19

dzbanuszek na śmietanę **29** 24

dziadek **3** 2

dziadkowie **2** 10

dział **47** 10

dział czasopism **47** 15

dział delikatesowy **14** 1

działo **48** 11

dzieci **2** 7

dziecko **2** 5

dziesięć centów **13** 29

dziewczyna—kowboj **81** 22

dziewczynka **2** 9

dzięcioł **64** 17

dziób **58** 5, **64** 3a, **64** 24a

dziurka do guzika **101** 8

dzwonko **11** 29

dżdżownica **62** 11

dżinsy **19** 6

dżokej **94** 21

dźwig **58** 6

dźwignia migaczy **50** 11

dźwignia przerzutki **52** 22

dźwignia zmiany
　　biegów **50** 17, **50** 24

edytor tekstu **83** 7

ekran **100** 14

elektronika **100**

elektrotechnik **84** 5

elektrownia **80** 20

elektryczność **80** 32

elektryk **85** 6

elipsa **79** 18

encyklopedia **47** 25

energia **80**

eukaliptus **61** 27

Europa **70** 3

fabryka **85**

fagot **98** 14

fajka **16** 26, **91** 34

fala **91** 24

farba **37** 31

farmer **81** 7

fartuch **16** 6

fasola **6** 13

fasola czarna **6** 14

fasolka szparagowa **6** 15

fazy Księżyca **74**

figa **9** 21

figury geometryczne **79**

filet **11** 28

filiżanka **13** 19, **29** 20

film **100**

film (na szpuli) **100** 17

film (w rolce) **100** 10

filtr papierowy **78** 16

filtr powietrza **51** 52

fiołek **60** 16

flaga **76** 1, **95** 9

flaming **64** 29

flara ostrzegawcza **51** 41

flądra **65** 7

flet **98** 13

Floryda **72** 9

foka **68** 12

fontanna **87** 14

football amerykański **92**

fortepian **98** 1

fotel biurowy **83** 17

fotel kubełkowy **50** 16

fotel na kółkach **39** 2

fotel odchylany **28** 16

fotele parteru **99** 12

fotograf **86** 4

fotografia **100, 100 B**

fotokopiarka **47** 18

frez ręczny **37** 37

frisbi **90** 13

frytki **18** 28

fryzjer damski **84** 10

fryzjer męski **84** 3

fundament **82** 11

furgon **49** 9

furgon pocztowy **46** 5

furgonetka **53** 26

gady **65**

galaktyka **74** 1

galaretka **18** 31

gałązka **61** 33a

ganek **27** 6

Ganges **71** 67

garaż **27** 2

garb **67** 33a

gardenia **60** 14

gardło **5** 59

garnek **30** 13

garnek na potrawkę **30** 14

garnitur trzyczęściowy **21** 40

gaśnica **42** 11

gaz ziemny **80** 29

gazeta **21** 48

gaziki **39** 25

gąbka **34** 7, **76** 11

gąsienica **63** 1

gejzer **80** 5

generator prądu **80** 21

Georgia **72** 10

gęś **64** 26

gibon **69** 15

gimnastyczka **94** 23

gimnastyka **94**

gips **39** 5

gitara **98** 11

gitara elektryczna **99** 26

gitarzysta basowy **99** 23

gitarzysta prowadzący **99** 25

glazura **34** 27

globus **47** 19

gładki **24** 20

głęboki talerz **13** 23

głębokość **79** 33

głośnik **28** 21, **76** 3

głośniki **100** 24

głowa **4**

gniazdko **36** 6

gniazdo **64** 31

gniazdo nasienne **8** 2b

golf **94**

gołąb **64** 1

goniec **85** 10, **86** 19

gorąco **25** 7

gorączka **40** 2

goryl **69** 17

gospodarstwo hodowlane **81**

gospodarstwo mleczne **81**

gospodarstwo rolne **81**

gotować **17** 4, **31** 16

gotować na parze **31** 12

góra **89** 19

Góry Skaliste **71** 40

grabić **26** 10

grabie **27** 30

gracz łapiący krótkie odbicia **93** 5

gracz przy drugiej bazie **93** 7

gracz przy pierwszej bazie **93** 8

gracz przy trzeciej bazie **93** 4

granat ręczny **48** 29

grapefruit **8** 7

grill **27** 22, **88** 12

grupa rockowa **99**

gruszka **8** 18

gruszka do betonu **49** 13

gry zespołowe **92**

gryzonie **66**

grzanka **18** 34

grządka **81** 18

grzebień **32** 6

grzechotka **33** 21

grzechotnik **65** 10

grzyb **7** 30

grzywa **67** 21a

gumka do ołówka **76** 21

guzik **20** 3, **101** 9

gwiazda **74** 4

gwint **37** 42b

gwizdek **90** 5

gwóźdź **37** 41

haczyk **36** 16

haft **101** 27

haftka **101** 14

halka **22** 10

hall **44** 2, **76** 11

hamak **27** 11

hamburger **18** 9

hamulec **50** 26, **52** 17

hamulec ręczny **50** 15, **52** 24

hangar **57** 17

harfa **98** 6

harmonijka ustna **98** 30

Hawaje **72** 11

helikopter **57** 2

hełm **42** 12

herbata **16** 15

hiacynt **60** 10

hiena **69** 30

Himalaje **19** 9, **71** 47

hipopotam **66** 14

hodowla **81**

hokej na lodzie **92**

holownik **58** 13

homar **11** 30, **62** 13

Huanghe **71** 68

huśtawka **33** 24

huśtawka na desce **87** 18

huśtawki krzesełkowe **87** 16

hydrant **42** 9

hydraulik **85** 1

Idaho **72** 12

igła **39** 26, **61** 34a, **101** 18

igła zespolona **100** 19

iguana **65** 13

Illinois **72** 13

ilości **12–13**

iluminator **58** 21

imadło **37** 36

indeks adresowy **83** 14

Indiana **72** 14

indyk **11** 23, **64** 20

informacja **47** 22

infekcja **40** 14

instrumenty **39** 13, **56** 14

instrumenty blaszane **98**

instrumenty muzyczne **98**

instrumenty perkusyjne **98**

instrumenty strunowe **98**

inwentarz **81** 12

Iowa **72** 15

irys **60** 11

iść **77** 8

jabłko **8** 2

jacht motorowy **59** 16

jadalnia **29**

jagnię **67** 24

jajko (sadzone) **18** 32

jajo **64** 13

Jangcy **71** 69

jaskier **60** 17

jasny **24** 9

jastrząb **64** 7

jaszczurka **65** 15

jaś **6** 16

jazda na łyżwach **94**

jechać **97** 13

jeleń **67** 26

jelita **5** 67

Jenisej **71** 65

jesień **26**

jeść **17** 1

jeżyna **8** 12

jeżozwierz **66** 11

jeździć na łyżwach **97** 9

jeździć na fali **97** 12

jeździec na koniu **87** 6

język **4** 41

Jowisz **74** 15

jubiler **84** 12

Jukon **71** 56

kabaczek zielony **7** 28

kabina **56** 19

kabina kontroli lotu **75** 10

kabina pilota **56** 13

kabura **43** 8

kaczka **11** 25, **64** 25

kadłub **57** 14

kajak **59** 17

kajdanki **43** 4

kajzerka **18** 19

kaktus **61** 40

kalafior **6** 1

kalendarz **83** 9

Kalifornia **72** 5

kalkulator **83** 19, **100** 34

kałamarnica **62** 5

kamera filmowa **100** 15

kamera wideo **100** 1

kamerzysta **86** 10

kamizelka **59** 1, **21** 39

kamizelka puchowa **19** 12

kanadyjka **59** 2

kanapa **28** 25

kanapka **16** 16

kanarek **64** 14

kangur **66** 3

kanion **88** 3

Kansas **72** 16

kantalupa **9** 36

kapelusz **19** 18

kapsułka **41** 5

kapusta **6** 3

kara **43**

karabin **48** 21

karaczan **63** 9

karczoch **6** 11

kardynał **64** 11

karetka **42** 6

karnisz **34** 1

Karolina Południowa **73** 40

Karolina Północna **73** 33

karta biblioteczna **47** 3

karta choroby **39** 10

karta dań **16** 7

karta katalogowa **47** 6

karta pocztowa **46** 17

karta wejścia na pokład **56** 18

karton **12** 1

karuzela **87** 5

kasa **15** 21

kasa biletowa **55** 19

kaseta **100** 26

kaseta na biżuterię **32** 4

kaseta wideo (taśma) **100** 3

kasjer **15** 22, **86** 15

kask **52** 7, **92** 6, **92** 14

kask roboczy **21** 28, **82** 4

kasztan **9** 32

katalog **47** 4

Kaukaz **71** 45

kawa **18** 35

kawałek **13** 22

kawałek (mydła) **13** 18

kawałek (pizzy) **13** 21

kąpielówki **91** 33

kąt ostry **79** 8

kąt prosty **79** 23

kąt rozwarty **79** 5

kciuk **4** 24

keczup **16** 4

kelner **16** 5

kelnerka **16** 2

kelnerka roznosząca koktaile **16** 32

Kentucky **72** 17

kieliszek do wina **29** 5

kieliszek na wodę **29** 6

kielnia **27** 27

kieł **66** 17b

kiełbasa **10** 7

kierowca autobusu **54** 3

kierowca ciężarówki **49** 16

kierownica **50** 8

kierownica (kolarska) **52** 2

kierownica turystyczna **52** 12

kierownik **83** 18

kieszeń **21** 41

kij do umieszczania piłeczki w
    dołku **94** 9

kij hokejowy **92** 18

kijanka **65** 16

kije **95** 5

kijek **94** 34, **95** 14

kilof **82** 13

kiosk z gazetami **45** 30

kiść bananów **9** 20

kiść winogron **8** 1

klakson **50** 12

klamka **50** 4

klapa **20** 1

klarnet **98** 16

klasa **76**

klawiatura **98** 1a, **100** 33

klej **37** 33, **76** 17

klema **51** 55

kleszcze **78** 28

klient **15** 17

klimatyzator **32** 11

klips **23** 15

klocek **33** 32

klon **61** 38

klucz nastawny **36** 10

klucz nastawny pojedyńczy **36** 12

kłódka **52** 13

knykieć **4** 22

koala **66** 1

kobieta **2** 1

kobra **65** 11

koc **32** 20

kociak **68** 5

kocioł **98** 21

kod pocztowy **46** 12

kogut **64** 21

kojec **33** 30

kokon **63** 2

kokos **8** 3

kolano **4** 19

kolba **6** 12a, **78** 2

kolczyk **23** 16, **23** 1

kolec **60** 18c, **66** 11a

kolej na jednej szynie **55** 29

kolejka dojazdowa **55** 14

kolejka linowa **55** 31

kolektor słoneczny **80** 17

koliber **64** 2

Kolorado **72** 6

kolumna kierownicza **50** 13

kołek **95** 13

kołnierz **20** 20

koło **52** 4, **79** 11

koło ratunkowe **90** 9

koło zapasowe **51** 39

kołonotatnik **76** 15

kołowrotek u wejścia **54** 12

kołyska **33** 26

komar **63** 13

kombajn **81** 17

kombi **50**

kombinerki **36** 19

kombinezon **21** 30

komedia muzyczna **99**

kometa **74** 2

komin **27** 9, **58** 18, **88** 22

kominek **28** 8

komoda **32** 30

komoda—toaletka **32** 9

komputer **76** 8, **83** 16

komputer osobisty **100** 31

komputery **100**

komunikacja **54–55**

konar **61** 35a

konduktor **54** 7

konewka **27** 16

konga **98** 20

Kongo **71** 62

koniczynka **53** 4

konie **81** 23

konik morski **65** 1

konserwacja **85**

konstelacja (Wielki Wóz) **74** 3

kontakt **32** 25

kontener **58** 7

kontrabas **98** 10

kontroler **86** 13

kontynenty **70**

konwojent **49** 10

koń **67** 21

końcówka **51** 55

kończyny przednie **66** 4c

kończyny tylne **66** 4a

kopać **26** 3, **96** 3

kopalnia węgla **80** 6

koparka **82** 26

kopczyk miotacza **93** 11

koperta **83** 31

koperta (lotnicza) **46** 16

kopiarka **83** 24

kopyto **67** 35b

kora **61** 35c

korba **36** 9

korek **16** 18, **34** 10, **78** 10

korkociąg **16** 17

koronka robiona igłą **101** 26

kort **94** 13

kort tenisowy **95**

koryto **81** 25

korzeń **61** 35d

kosiarka do trawy **27** 12

kosić **26** 6

kosmetyki **23**

kostium kąpielowy **90** 18

kostka **5** 49, **5** 52, **90** 11a

kosz **92** 20

kosz na bieliznę **35** 29

kosz na śmieci **34** 13, **44** 15, **87** 11

kosz z pokrywką **34** 28

koszula **21** 46

koszula flanelowa **19** 3

koszula nocna **22** 21

koszulka **22** 9

koszulka gimnastyczna **20** 13

koszyk **14** 8, **88** 13

koszykówka **92**

kot **68** 4

kotlety baranie **10** 15

kotlety schabowe **18** 15

kotwica **58** 24

kowboj **81** 21

koza **67** 28

kółka **24** 2

kółka do nauki **52** 1

krab **11** 36, **62** 9

kran **16** 20

krawat **21** 47

krawężnik **45** 26

krawiec **84** 6

krążek **92** 17

kreda **76** 10

kredens **29** 2

krem do golenia **23** 22

krewetka **11** 31, **62** 8

kręgle **94** 5

krochmal w spray'u **35** 21
kroić **31** 6
kroić **31** 9
krokiet **18** 25
krokus **60** 9
krokwie **82** 1
kromka (chleba) **13** 21
krople do oczu **41** 10
krowa **67** 32
krowy mleczne **81** 11
królik **66** 13
krótki **24** 1
krótki rękaw **20** 21
kruche ciasto z truskawkami **18** 26
kruk **64** 3
krzesło **29** 17
krzesło ratownika **90** 8
krzewy **61** 41
krzywa **79** 3
książeczka **13** 17
księgarnia **45** 18
księgowy **86** 18
księgozbiór podręczny **47** 21
Księżyc **74** 9
ksylofon **98** 31
ku **103** 4
kubełek **12** 6
kucharz **16** 1
kuchenka **30** 30, **89** 25
kuchnia **30**
kuchnia mikrofalowa **30** 23
kucyk **67** 20
kukurydza **60** 24
kukurydza (kaczan) **6** 12
kula **48** 26, **94** 6
kule **39** 7
kura **64** 23
kurczak **11** 24
kurczak (cały) **11** 16
kurczak smażony **18** 29
kurek ciepłej wody **34** 17
kurek zimnej wody **34** 18
kurtka **19** 24
kurtyna **99** 1
kuweta **37** 28

kuzyn **3** 7
kwadrat **79** 9
kwiaciarz **84** 11
kwiaty **60**
laboratorium fizyczno-chemiczne **78**
lacrosse **92**
lada chłodnicza **15** 16
lakier do paznokci **23** 25
lalka **33** 28
lama **66** 15
lamówka **101** 12
lampa **28** 28
lampa błyskowa **100** 7
lampart **68** 1
lasy **89** 32
latarka **35** 3
latarnia **89** 29
latarnia morska **58** 14
latarnia uliczna **45** 29
latawiec **91** 22
lato **26**
lądowanie na Księżycu **75**
lądownik **75** 7
leczenie **41**
lejek **78** 17
lekarstwa **41**
lekarz **39** 11
leki **41**
lekkoatletyka **94**
Lena **71** 66
lew **68** 3
lewy gracz w polu **93** 1
lewy osłaniający **93** 26
lewy przechwytujący **93** 25
leżak **90** 20
leżanka **27** 24
leżenie **41** 1
lichtarz **29** 28
lilia **60** 3
limona **8** 10
lina **89** 23
lina holownicza **59** 11
linia autowa **93** 9
linia główna **95** 4
linia prosta **79** 1

linia serwisowa **95** 3
linie **79**
linie elektryczne **80** 24
linie prostopadłe **79** 2
linie równoległe **79** 4
linijka **76** 23
linka **52** 23
lis **68** 6
list **46** 7
liść **61** 36a
lodówka **30** 19, **91** 41
lody w waflu **18** 36
lora samochodowa **49** 17
lornetka **90** 7
lotnia **57** 6
lotnictwo **48** 19
lotnik **48** 20
lotniskowiec **48** 4
loża **99** 11
ludzie **2**
lufa **48** 23
Luizjana **72** 18
luk bagażowy **57** 12
lusterko boczne **50** 2
lusterko wsteczne **50** 7
lustro **32** 5
luźny **24** 4
łabędź **64** 28
ładownia **58** 8, **75** 9
ładunek **58** 10
łańcuch **52** 18
łańcuchy górskie **71**
łańcuszek z wisiorkiem **23** 5
łapać **96** 4
łapacz **93** 16
ława **28** 26
ława przysięgłych **43** 20
ławka **44** 14, **76** 16, **87** 10
łazienka **34**
łącznica telefoniczna **83** 3
łeb **37** 42a
łodyga **60** 1a
łokieć **4** 8
łopata **27** 31, **67** 35a
łopatka **27** 21, **90** 17

łoś amerykański **67** 35

łódź podwodna **48** 7

łódź ratunkowa **58** 19, **90** 10

łódź rybacka **58** 1

łódź wiosłowa **59** 23

łóżeczko dziecięce **33** 4

łóżko **32** 21

łuk **79** 16

łydka **4** 20

łyżka **29** 8

łyżwa **94** 26

łyżwy **19** 15

magazyn ilustrowany **47** 16

magnes **78** 27

magnetowid **100** 4

magnolia **61** 29

Maine **72** 19

majster **82** 5

majteczki bikini **22** 11

majtki **22** 12

malarz **85** 7

malina **8** 16

malować **26** 1

małpa **69** 14

mały **24** 7

mały palec **5** 55

małż **11** 32

mandolina **98** 4

mango **8** 5

mapa świata **70–71**

marchewka **7** 32

Mars **74** 14

Maryland **72** 20

marynarka **20** 2, **48** 13

marynarz **48** 14

maska **91** 35, **92** 3, **92** 15

masło **18** 18

Massachusetts **72** 21

maszt **59** 8

maszyna do pisania **82** 10

maszyna do szycia **101** 1

maszyna startowa **95** 20

maszynista **55** 15

maszynistka **83** 6

maszynka do golenia **23** 20

maść **41** 9

mata **34** 12

matematyka **79**

materac **32** 17

materac nadmuchiwany **91** 26

materiał **101** 4

matka **3** 4

mąż **2** 3, **3** 12

mechanik pokładowy **56** 17

mechanik samochodowy **84** 2

meduza **62** 12

meksykański placek **18** 24

melba **18** 23

melon wonny **9** 35

melonowiec **8** 6

menzurka **78** 25

Merkury **74** 11

meteor **74** 5

meteorolog **86** 1

metr krawiecki **101** 15

metro **54**

mewa **64** 4

mężczyzna **2** 2

mgliście **25** 12

miarka taśmowa **36** 21

miasto **44–45**

Michigan **72** 22

miecz **59** 6

miecznik **65** 3

mieszać **31** 1

mieszanka warzywna **18** 16

miejsce biwakowe **88**

miejsce dla świadka **43** 18

miejsce do cumowania **59** 19

miejsce do siedzenia **54** 2

mięczaki **11**

międzypiętrze **99** 13

mięsień **5** 62

mięso **10**

mięso na gulasz **10** 4

mięso przegrzebka **11** 35

migacze **51** 50

migdał **9** 31

mikrofilm **47** 13

mikroskop **78** 30

mikser **30** 12

Minicam™ **100** 2

Minnesota **72** 23

minutnik **78** 13

miotła **35** 7

miska **13** 23

Missisipi **71** 58, **72** 24

Missouri **73** 25

miś **33** 3

mleko **14** 5

młode **67** 27

młot pneumatyczny **82** 22

młotek **36** 13, **43** 12

młotek gumowy **36** 11

mobil **33** 2

modelka **86** 5

modliszka **63** 7

moduł dowodzenia **75** 8

mokasyn **21** 42

mokro **25** 15

monety **13** 26

monitor **100** 32

Montana **73** 26

monter **82** 17

morela **9** 25

mors **68** 11

morza **70**

Morze Arabskie **70** 30

Morze Baffina **70** 16

Morze Bałtyckie **70** 22

Morze Barentsa **70** 23

Morze Beauforta **70** 15

Morze Beringa **70** 34

Morze Czarne **70** 26

Morze Czerwone **70** 29

Morze Japońskie **70** 36

Morze Karaibskie **70** 20

Morze Karskie **70** 31

Morze Kaspijskie **70** 27

Morze Łaptiewów **70** 33

Morze Ochockie **70** 35

Morze Południowochińskie **70** 39

Morze Północne **70** 21

Morze Śródziemne **70** 24

Morze Wschodniochińskie **70** 38

Morze Żółte **70** 37
motek **101** 24
motel **90** 3
motocykl **52** 30, **53** 19
motopompa **42** 3
motorówka **59** 13
motyl **63** 3
moździerz **48** 28
mól **63** 21
mózg **5** 57
mrówka **63** 12
mrówkojad **66** 5
mrożonki **14** 2
mroźnie **25** 16
mucha **63** 18
mula **11** 34
mundur **21** 45
muszla **62** 1a, **91** 48
muszla klozetowa **34** 29
muszla koncertowa **87** 2
musztarda **18** 1
muzyk **99** 10
muzyk grający na klawiaturach **99** 22
muzyka **99**
mydelniczka **34** 6
mydło **34** 15
myjka **30** 11, **34** 22
myjka do podłogi (z gąbką) **35** 6
mysz **66** 9
myto **53** 27
na **102** 5, **103** 9
na wierzchu **102** 10
na wprost **102** 6
nabój **48** 27
naczelne **69**
nakrętka **37** 39
nakrywać do stołu **17** 8
nalepka **46** 21
naleśniki **18** 5
nalewać **31** 4
namiot **89** 24
naparstek **101** 21
napastnik cofnięty **93** 34
napastnik dalszy **93** 33
napastnik flankujący **93** 31

napastnik skrzydłowy **93** 24, **93** 30
napastnik środkowy **93** 32
napełniać **26** 9
napiwek **55** 22
napoje **14** 14
napój alkoholowy **16** 22
napój orzeźwiający **16** 11
naprawa **38**
naprawy **85**
narciarstwo biegowe **94**
narciarz **94** 35
narciarz wodny **59** 10
narta **95** 17
narty **94** 33
narządy wewnętrzne **5**
narzuta **32** 23
naszyjnik **23** 6
nauczyciel **76** 4
nauszniki **19** 10
nawiew **50** 21
Nebraska **73** 27
nektarynka **8** 17
Neptun **74** 18
nerka **5** 70
nerkowiec **9** 27
Nevada **73** 28
New Hampshire **73** 29
New Jersey **73** 30
niedźwiedź czarny **69** 21
niedźwiedź polarny **69** 22
niedźwiedź
     północnoamerykański **69** 23
niedźwiedzie **69**
nietoperz **66** 4d
Niger **71** 61
Nil **71** 63
niski **24** 12
nocnik **33** 33
noga **4** 17, **11** 20
nos **4** 36
nosić **26** 16
nosorożec **66** 16
nosze **39** 12
notatnik służbowy **83** 25
nowy **24** 13

Nowy Jork **73** 32
Nowy Meksyk **73** 31
nozdrze **4** 37
nożyczki **101** 17
nożyczki z ząbkami **101** 5
nów **74** 26
nóż **29** 15
nóżka **52** 9
numer budynku **45** 24
numer rejestracyjny **50** 28
nurkować **97** 14
nuty **98** 2
Ob **71** 64
obcas **20** 5
obiektyw **100** 6
obierać **31** 5
obok **102** 11, **103** 2
obozowisko **89**
obój **98** 15
obrączka **23** 4
obraz **28** 5
obrus **29** 16
obsługiwać **17** 3
obwód **79** 17
Ocean Indyjski **70** 13
Ocean Lodowaty **70** 8
oceany **70**
ochraniacz na głowę **94** 14
ochraniacz **30** 34
ochrona **56**
od **103** 5
odbijać **97** 11
odbiornik **100** 21
odbitki **100** 11
odciski palców **43** 24
odgarniać **26** 13
odgrodzenie **16** 9
odkurzacz **35** 16
odkurzać **38** 14
odprawa na lotnisku **56**
odrzutowiec **57** 18
odtwarzacz płyt kompaktowych **100** 28
odważnik **78** 5
odznaka **43** 5
odźwierny **85** 11

ogień **28** 9, **42** 5
ognisko obozowe **89** 31
ogon **57** 10, **65** 3a, **66** 4
ogonek **8** 2a
ogórek **7** 20
ogórek konserwowy **18** 8
ogrodniczki **21** 30
ogrodnik **85** 3
Ohio **73** 35
ojciec **3** 5
okienko **46** 15
okienko z żetonami **54** 13
okiennica **27** 8
Oklahoma **73** 36
okno **27** 7
oko **5**
okulary **21** 44
okulary ochronne **78** 12, **94** 28
okulary słoneczne **90** 14
olej napędowy **80** 34
olej silnikowy **80** 33
olejek do opalania **91** 39
oliwić **38** 12
oliwka **33** 6
ołówek **76** 24
ołówek do brwi **23** 26
omułek **62** 3
opakowanie **12** 4
opalający się **90** 19
oparzenie **40** 18
opaska **20** 12
operacja **41** 2
opieka dentystyczna **39**
opieka medyczna **39**
opiekacz **30** 33
opiekacz do grzanek **30** 16
opiekać **31** 13
opłata za przejazd **55** 21
opona **50** 37, **52** 28
optyk **84** 9
orangutan **69** 18
orbita **74** 21
orchidea **60** 12
Oregon **73** 37
organy **98** 29

orkiestra **99** 6
orzech laskowy **9** 30
orzech włoski **9** 29
orzechy **9**
orzeł **64** 5
orzeszek ziemny **9** 28
osa **63** 20
osioł **67** 23
osłaniający skrzydło **93** 30
ostatnia kwadra **74** 25
ostrokrzew **61** 37
ostrosłup **79** 25
ostryga **11** 33, **62** 2
ostrze **94** 27
ośmiornica **62** 6
otwarty **24** 15
otwierać **31** 3
otwieracz do butelek **30** 6
otwieracz do konserw **30** 4
otwierany dach **51** 44
otwór przelewowy **34** 9
owady **63**
owca **67** 25
owce **81** 10
owczarek **69** 28
owies **60** 23
owoce **8-9**
owoce cytrusowe **8**
owoce jagodowe **8**
owoce morza **11**
pacha **4** 10
pachołek **58** 26, **82** 19
pacjent **39** 20
paczka **12** 5, **13** 16, **46** 19
padać **96** 7
pająk **63** 16
pajęczyna **63** 15
palec mały **4** 28
palec wskazujący **4** 25
palec serdeczny **4** 27
palec środkowy **4** 26
palec u nogi **5** 54
paletka **94** 18
paliwo do silników odrzutowych **80** 31
palma **61** 26

palnik **30** 29
palnik Bunsena **78** 20
pałeczki **98** 19a
pałka **43** 9, **92** 5
pancernik **48** 5, **66** 2
panda **69** 20
pantofle ranne **22** 18
papier milimetrowy **78** 11
papier ścierny **37** 27
papier toaletowy **34** 30
papieros **16** 31
papryka **7** 22
papuga **64** 16
papużka **64** 15
paragon **15** 20
Parana **71** 60
parasol plażowy **90** 21
parasolka **20** 24
park osiedlowy **87**
parking **45** 19
parkometr **45** 20
parówka **18** 2
pas **4** 13
pas bezpieczeństwa **50** 23
pas elastyczny **22** 15
pas lewy **53** 5
pas startowy **57** 19
pas środkowy **53** 6
pasażer **54** 6, **55** 25
pasażerski liniowiec oceaniczny **58** 27
pasek **20** 16
pasek do podwiązek **22** 14
pasek do zegarka **23** 11
pasek klinowy **51** 53
pasikonik **63** 6
pasta do zębów **34** 16
pastwisko **81** 6
patelnia **30** 5
patio **27** 17
paw **64** 18
pawian **69** 19
paznokieć **4** 23, **5** 56
pazur **68** 2a, **69** 29a
pączek **60** 18a
pchać **26** 12

pęcherz **5** 72

pedał **39** 18, **52** 19

pedał gazu **50** 27

pędzel do malowania **37** 30

pędzelek **76** 18

pelikan **64** 24

pełnia Księżyca **74** 24

Pensylwania **73** 38

perfumy **23** 27

perkusista **99** 27

peron **54** 11

personel **48**

peryskop **48** 8

pestka **8** 8c, **9** 37a

petunia **60** 7

pianka **91** 38

piasek **91** 31

piaskownica **87** 13

piccolo **98** 12

pick-up **49** 4

pić **17** 2

piec **31** 14

piechota morska **48** 17

piecyk **30** 32

pieczeń **10** 3, **10** 8

pieczony ziemniak **18** 20

piekarnia **44** 6

piekarz **84** 8

pielęgniarka **39** 19

pieluszki jednorazowe **33** 12

pieluszki płócienne **33** 13

pieniądze **12–13**

pień **61** 35b

pieprzniczka **29** 9

pierś **4** 12, **11** 21

pierścień **74** 16a

pierścionek **23** 2

pierścionek zaręczynowy **23** 3

pierwsza kwadra **74** 23

pies myśliwski **69** 26

pieszy **44** 12

pięć centów **13** 28

pięta **5** 50

pigułka **41** 7

pikowanie **101** 32

piła **36** 8

piła mechaniczna **27** 25

piła tarczowa **36** 20

piłeczka **94** 12

piłeczka golfowa **94** 7

piłeczka ping pongowa **94** 19

piłeczka ręczna **94**

piłka **94** 30

piłka do koszykówki **92** 21

piłka do metalu **36** 18

piłka do siatkówki **92** 22

piłka footbolowa **92** 13

piłka miękka **92** 10

piłka nożna **92, 92** 26

piłka plażowa **90** 11

piłka tenisowa **94** 1

pilnik do paznokci **23** 24

pilot **28** 17, **56** 15

pinceta **78** 32

pinezka **76** 25

pingwin **64** 27

pionierki **19** 9

pióro **64** 7a

pipeta **78** 14

pirs **58** 3

pisać **77** 7

pisać na maszynie **77** 10

pisarz **86** 7

pisklę **64** 22

pisma przychodzące **83** 12

pistolet maszynowy **48** 25

piwo **16** 23

pizza **18** 30

piżama **22** 19

plac budowy **82**

plac zabaw **87** 15

planetoida **74** 20

planety **74**

plany **82** 6

plaster **39** 4

plasterek (cytryny) **13** 21

platforma **49** 18

plaża **90–91**

plecak **19** 4

plecak ze stelażem **89** 28

plecy **4** 11

pluszowe zwierzątko **33** 27

Pluton **74** 19

płacić **17** 7

płaski **24** 12

płaskowyż **88** 1

płaszcz **19** 20, **42** 13

płaszcz kąpielowy **22** 20

płaszcz przeciwdeszczowy **21** 38

płaszczka **65** 6

płatek **60** 18b

płazy **65**

płetwa **65** 3b, **68** 12a

płetwy **91** 36

płody rolne **14** 9

płomień **29** 26, **78** 21

płot **81** 9

płuco **5** 63

płyg śnieżny **49** 5

płyn do mycia naczyń **30** 10

płyn do płukania **35** 27

płyn po goleniu **23** 21

płyta kompaktowa **100** 27

płytka Petriego **78** 3

płyty **100** 23

pływak **91** 28

pobocze **53** 22

pochmurna **25** 2

pociąg **55**

poczta **44** 9

poczta w U.S.A. **46**

pod **102** 8, **103** 11

podawac **17** 9, **96** 5

podbicie **5** 51

podbierak **88** 9

podbite oko **40** 5

podbródek **4** 3

podejrzany **43** 3

podeszwa **20** 6

podium **99** 7

podjazd **27** 1

podkładka **37** 40

podkolanówki **22** 16

podkoszulka **21** 29, **22** 1

podlewać **26** 5

podłoga **32** 29
podłokietnik **50** 3
podnieść (rękę) **77** 1
podnośnik **51** 38
podręcznik **76** 26
podróż drogą **53**
podróż lotnicza **56**
podróżny **56** 3
podsądny **43** 23
podstawa **79** 7
podstawki **16** 27
poduszka **28** 24, **32** 16
poduszka do igieł **101** 3
poduszka elektryczna **41** 3
podwórko **81** 8
podwórko za domem **27**
podwozie **57** 15
pogoda **25**
poinsecja **60** 15
pojazd holowniczy **49** 2
pojazdy i sprzęt **48**
pojemnik **12** 2, **30** 15
pojemnik na bagaż **56** 21
pojemnik na lód **30** 21
pojemnik na opłatę **54** 5
pojemnik na śmieci **35** 31
pojemnik z aerozolem **13** 24
pojemniki **12–13**
pokład **58** 22
pokój dzienny **28**
pokój dziecięcy **33**
pokój gospodarczy **35**
pokrewieństwa **2**
pokrywa silnika **51** 47
pokrywka **30** 9
polano **28** 10
pole footballowe **93**
pole (pszenicy) **81** 16
pole punktowe **93** 23
pole serwisowe **95** 1
polerować **38** 3
policjant **43** 6
policjant drogowy **44** 10
policzek **4** 35
połówka **79** 30

połówka kurczaka **11** 17
południe **71** 72
Południowy Atlantyk **70** 12
Południowy Pacyfik **70** 10
pomarańcza **8** 8
pomidor **7** 19
pomiędzy **102** 4
pomieszczenia dla załogi **75** 11
pomieszczenie biurowe **83** 5
pomieszczenie dla drużyn **93** 13
pomoc stomatologiczna **39** 14
pomoc domowa **85** 8
pomocnik **16** 3, **29** 29
pompka **52** 21
ponad **102** 2, **103** 6
pończochy **22** 6
poniżej **102** 3
popielniczka **16** 29
poprzez **103** 1, **103** 6
popularne dania **18**
porcelana **29** 1
porcja (lodów) **13** 18
poręcz **28** 11
port **58**
portfel **20** 9
posterunek policji **43**
postój taksówek **55** 28
posypywać piaskiem **26** 14
pośladki **4** 15
pośrednik w handlu
    nieruchomościami **85** 5
powieka **5** 45
powłoczka na poduszkę **32** 15
powóz konny **55** 33
poziomica **82** 3
pożarnictwo **42**
półhalka **22** 8
półka **14** 6, **47** 17, **47** 26
półka nad kominkiem **28** 7
półka na książki **83** 20
północ **71** 71
Północny Atlantyk **70** 11
Północny Pacyfik **70** 9
prace domowe **38**
prace ręczne **101**

pracownicy biznesu **86**
pracownik oczyszczania miasta **49** 7
pracownik stacji **53** 12
pracownik transportowy **49** 12
prać **38** 16
pralka **35** 30
prasować **38** 11
prawy gracz w polu **93** 3
prawy osłaniający **93** 28
prawy pas **53** 7
prawy przechwytujący **93** 29
prezenter dziennika **86** 2
pręty uranowe **80** 15
probówka **78** 9
produkty nabiałowe **14** 4
produkty spożywcze **15** 24
produkty w puszkach **14** 13
program kosmiczny **75**
programista komputerów **86** 16
programy **99** 17
projektant mody **86** 6
projektor **100** 16
prokurator **43** 17
prom **58** 17
prom kosmiczny **75**
promień **79** 14
propan **80** 30
prostokąt **79** 19
proszek do prania **35** 25
proszek do szorowania **35** 9
protokolant **43** 14
protokół **43** 15
prowadzić **97** 15
prywatny odrzutowiec **57** 3
pryzmat **78** 1
przeciwprostokątna **79** 24
przedłużacz **36** 5
przedmioty gospodarstwa
    domowego **15** 15
przedramię **4** 9
przedziałek **4** 31
przegrzebek **62** 10
przegub **4** 21
przejście **14** 10, **56** 23
przejście dla pieszych **44** 4

przekaz pieniężny **46** 18
przekąski **15** 18
przekątna **79** 20
przekładnia automatyczna **50**
przekładnia ręczna **50**
przełyk **5** 61
przestępstwo **43**
przestrzeń kosmiczna **74**
przesyłka Poczty Ekspresowej **46** 23
przesyłki **46** 2
przeszkoda **95** 6
prześcieradło **32** 19
prześwietlenie **39** 1
przetykacz do zlewów **35** 14
przez **103** 8
przeziębienie **40** 11
przezrocza **100** 12
przędza **101** 31
przód **57** 8
przy **102** 1
przybory toaletowe i kosmetyczne **23**
przycinać **26** 8
przyczepa kampingowa **53** 10
przyimki opisowe **102**
przyimki ruchu **103**
przykrycie na nogi **32** 22
przypalać **17** 14
przyrząd do usuwania zszywek **83** 29
przysięgli **43** 21
przystanek autobusowy **44** 13
pstrąg **65** 2
psy **69**
pszczoła **63** 19
pszenica **60** 22
ptaki **64**
publiczność **99** 15
pudełko **13** 12
pudło na narzędzia **36** 23
pudło z zabawkami **33** 29
pułapka na myszy **35** 32
pułapka piaskowa **95** 11
pulpety **18** 11
punkt zamarzania **25** 11
puree z ziemniaków **18** 17
Pustynia Atakama **71** 50

Pustynia Gobi **71** 54
Pustynia Mojave **71** 48
Pustynia Painted **71** 49
Pustynia Rub al-Chali **71** 52
Pustynia Takla Makan **71** 53
pustynie **71**
puszka **12** 10
puzon **98** 23
rachunek **16** 14, **55** 24
racquetball **94**
radio **50** 18
rafineria **80** 12
rajstopy **22** 5
rajtuzy **19** 14
rakieta **75** 13, **92** 16, **94** 2,
    94 29
rama **28** 4
rama damki **52** 3
rama męska **52** 11
ramiączko **32** 2
ramię **4** 6, **4** 7, **100** 20
ratownictwo **42**
ratownik **90** 6
rąbać **26** 11
rąbek **101** 11
rdzeń **80** 14
rdzeń kręgowy **5** 58
reaktor atomowy **80** 13
recepcjonistka **86** 17
reflektor punktowy **99** 4
reflektory **51** 48
regał **28** 19, **47** 11
rekin **65** 5
reperować **38** 10
reporter **86** 11
restauracja rodzinna **16**
rewers **47** 12
rewolwer **43** 7
ręcznik **34** 23
ręcznik kąpielowy **34** 24, **90** 15
ręcznik papierowy **35** 23
ręka **4** 6
rękawica **27** 20, **92** 4, **92** 12,
    94 11, **94** 15
rękawice robocze **27** 26

rękawiczki **19** 1
rękawiczki z jednym palcem **19** 11
Rhode Island **73** 39
ring **94** 17
Rio Grande **71** 57
robaczek świętojański **63** 17
robota szydełkowa **101** 28
robotnik **85** 12
robtonik budowlany **82** 14
roboty drogowe **82**
robótka na drutach **101** 22
robótki z użyciem igły **101**
rodzaje przesyłek **46**
rodzice **2** 6
rodzina **3**
rodzynek **9** 24
rogatka **53** 27
roleta **33** 1
rolka **12** 11
rolnictwo **81**
rondel **30** 8
rośliny **60–61**
rośliny domowe **61** 39
rośliny trujące **61**
rower **52** 15
rower terenowy **52** 8
rowery **52**
rowerzysta **90** 4
rozbijać **31** 7
rozedrzeć **77** 9
rozgwiazda **62** 7
rozkład jazdy **55** 20
rozpryskiwacz **27** 13
rożek **62** 1b
rożek angielski **98** 26
róg **44** 3, **66** 16a
równik **71** 70
równoważnia **94** 24
róż **23** 32
róża **60** 18
ruchomy punkt żywienia **49** 8
rudzik **64** 9
rufa **58** 11
rumianek **60** 5
rura **35** 18

rura gumowa **78** 18
rura wydechowa **52** 33
rusztowanie **82** 7
ryba **11** 26
rybak **58** 2
ryby **65**
rynna **94** 3
rynna pozioma **27** 10
rynna ściekowa **27** 18
rysować **77** 11
rysunki techniczne **82** 6
ryż **60** 21
rzeki **71**
rzepa **7** 34
rzeżucha **6** 5
rzeźnik **84** 13
rzęsy **5** 46
rzodkiewka **7** 29
rzucać **97** 10
rzutnik **76** 27
rzutnik przezroczy **100** 13
sad **81** 1
sadzawka (dla kaczek) **87** 8
sadzić **26** 4
Sahara **71** 51
saksofon **98** 24
sala szkolna **76**
salamandra **65** 14
salaterka **29** 25
sałata zielona **6** 6
sałatka mieszana **10** 13
samochód do przeprowadzek **49** 11
samochód kempingowy **53** 16
samochód osobowy **53** 15
samochód sportowy **53** 17
samochód terenowy **48** 9
samochody **50–51**
samolot myśliwski **48** 1
samolot śmigłowy **57** 7
sandał **20** 19
sanitariusz **39** 8, **42** 7
satacja obsługi **53** 11
satelita komunikacyjny **75** 2
satelita meteorologiczny **75** 3
Saturn **74** 16

sąd **43**
scena **99** 5
schabowy **10** 9
schody **28** 12
schody ewakuacyjne **42** 4
schowek **50** 20
sedan dwudrzwiowy **51**
segregator szufladowy **83** 21
sekator **27** 29
sekretarka **83** 11
sekwoja **61** 25
seler naciowy **6** 10
serce **5** 64
serwetka **29** 14
serwować **96** 2
sędzia **43** 10, **92** 1, **92** 22, **93** 1,
    94 16
siano (w beli) **81** 13
siatka **27** 19, **92** 23, **95** 2
siatka druciana **78** 6
siatkówka **92**
siedzenie dla dziecka **50** 33
siedzenie tylne **50** 32
Sierra Madre **71** 42
silnik **51, 52** 32
silnik doczepny **59** 12
silnik odrzutowy **57** 11
silos **81** 4
siły lądowe **48** 15
siły zbrojne **48**
siodełko **52** 16
siodło **94** 20
siostra **3** 10
siostrzenica **3** 14
siostrzeniec **3** 13
sitko prysznica **34** 4
skafander **19** 8
skafander kosmiczny **75** 6
skakać **96** 8
skaleczenie **40** 16
skała **89** 21
skałki **88** 11
skarpety **22** 17
składać **38** 1
składzik na narzędzia **27** 28

sklep warzywny **45** 28
skoroszyt **76** 14
skorpion **63** 8
skorupa **65** 18a
skorupiaki **11**
skórka **8** 8b, **9** 20a, **9** 37b
skrzela **65** 3c
skrzydełko **11** 22
skrzydło **57** 9, **63** 4a, **64** 1a
skrzynka na listy **46** 1
skrzynka pocztowa **46** 6
skrzypce **98** 7
skrzyżowanie **44** 11
skunks **68** 8
skurzawka **35** 2
skuter **52** 29
slipy **22** 3
słoik **12** 9
słomka **16** 10
słoneczna **25** 4
słonecznik **60** 19
słoń **66** 17
Słońce **74** 7, **80** 3
słownik **47** 24
słuchać **77** 6
słuchawki **100** 29
słuchawki z mikrofonem **83** 2
słup bramkowy **93** 35
słup energetyczny **80** 26
słupy wysokiego napięcia **80** 23
służba domowa **85**
smarować **17** 11
smażyć **31** 15
smoczek **33** 18, **33** 22
smyczek **98** 7a
softball **92**
solniczka **29** 10
sonda kosmiczna **75** 4
sos do sałaty **10** 12
sosna **61** 34
sowa **64** 6
sójka amerykańska **64** 8
spadochron **48** 6
spaghetti **18** 10
spaniel **69** 24

spinacz **83** 28

spinacze do bielizny **35** 20

spinka do krawata **23** 14

spinki do mankietów **23** 12

spirytus **39** 22

spluwaczka **39** 16

spływ tratwą **89**

spodek **29** 21

spodnie **20** 4

spodnie od dresu **20** 10

spodnie sztruksowe **21** 27

sporty indywidualne **94**

sporty wodne **59**

spódnica **21** 36

sprężarka **53** 13

sprężyny **32** 18

sprzączka **20** 17

sprzedawca **86** 12

sprzedawca uliczny **87** 3

sprzedawca warzyw **84** 7

sprzęgło **50** 25

sprzęt foniczny **100**

spust **48** 22

spychacz **82** 27

ssaki **66–69**

ssaki bezzębne **66**

ssaki kopytne **66**

ssaki latające **66**

ssaki wodne **68**

ssawki do odkurzacza **35** 17

stacja **55** 18

stacja kosmiczna **75** 1

stacja metra **44** 16

stacyjka **50** 14

stanik **22** 13

stanowisko kasowe **15** 26

Stany Zjednoczone Ameryki **72–73**

start **57**

stary **24** 14

statek (kontenerowy) **58** 9

statek kosmiczny **75**

statki powietrzne **57**

statyw **100** 9

statyw z pierścieniem **78** 19

stempel **46** 9

ster **59** 5

stereofoniczny magnetofon
  kasetowy **100** 25

sterowiec **57** 5

stetoskop **39** 9

steward **56** 20

stłuczenie **40** 17

stodoła **81** 5

stojak **47** 17, **78** 8

stojak na rowery **52** 14

stolarz **85** 2

stołek **78** 34

stołek barowy **16** 25

stolik do przebierania **33** 9

stolik nocny **32** 27

stolik opuszczany **56** 22

stolik podręczny **28** 29

stonoga **63** 22

stopa **5**

stopień **28** 13

stożek **79** 28

stół **29** 7, **78** 24

stół do badania **39** 6

stół na piknik **88** 15

stół warsztatowy **36** 22

strach na wróble **81** 19

strażak **42** 10

strażnik **56** 9, **86** 14

strażnik parku **88** 5

strażnik sądowy **43** 19

strąk **6** 17a

strój **92** 9

strug **37** 32

strumień **88** 6

struna **98** 10a

struś **64** 12

strzelać **97** 16

strzykawka **39** 27

sucharek **18** 27

sucho **25** 14

sufit **28** 2

sukienka **20** 22

sumak jadowity **61** 44

supermarket **14–15**

suseł **66** 8

suspensorium **22** 4

suszarka **30** 2, **35** 24

suszone owoce **9**

sweter z golfem **19** 13

sweter z półgolfem **19** 7

sweter w serek **19** 23

sygnalizacja świetlna **45** 21

sygnał **52** 5

sygnatura **47** 7

syn **3** 16

syntetyzator **99** 21

sypialnia **32**

syrop **18** 6

szafa grająca **16** 12

szafa w ścianie **32** 3

szafka **30** 22, **76** 6

szal **19** 19

szampon **34** 8

szatkować **31** 11

szczebel **33** 5, **82** 9

szczęka **4** 38

szczeniak **69** 27

szczotka do paznokci **34** 20

szczotka do włosów **32** 7

szczotka do zębów **34** 21

szczotka klozetowa **34** 31

szczur **66** 7

szczypce **62** 13a, **78** 29

szczyt **89** 20

szczyt długi **32** 14

szczyt krótki **32** 24

szerokość **79** 35

sześcian **79** 27

szew **101** 10

szkatułka **32** 4

szkiełko **78** 31

szklanka **13** 20

szkło powiększające **78** 15

szlifierka elektryczna **37** 26

szmaty **35** 4

szminka **23** 29

sznur **32** 26a, **54** 1

sznur do bielizny **35** 19

sznur paciorków **23** 7

sznurek **46** 20

sznurowadło **20** 7
szop **68** 7
szorować **38** 2
szorty **20** 14, **22** 2
szpachla **36** 14
szparagi **6** 18
szpatułka **40** 12a
szpilka **23** 8, **101** 20
szpilka do krawata **23** 13
szpinak **6** 8
szprycha **52** 26
szpulka nici **101** 2
sztućce **29** 22
sztuka **86**
sztyft **23** 18
szufla **82** 15
szuflada **47** 5
szwagier **3** 11
szwagierka **3** 8
szwy **39** 21
szyb **80** 10
szyb naftowy **80** 1
szyba przednia **51** 45
szybkościomierz **50** 10
szybowiec **57** 4
szycie **101**
szydełko **101** 29
szyja **4** 4
szympans **69** 16
szynka **10** 12
szyszka **61** 34b
ściana **28** 3
ścieg **101** 19
ścielić **38** 8
ścierać kurze **38** 15
ścierka do naczń **30** 18
ścierki **35** 4
ścienżka do jazdy na koniu **87** 7
ścisk stolarski **36** 2
śledź **89** 30
ślimak **62** 1
ślimak nagi **62** 4
śliniak **33** 20
śliwka **9** 22, **9** 34
ślusarz **85** 4

śmieciarka **49** 6
śmietniczka **35** 8
śmigło **57** 2a
śniadaniówka **21** 31
śniegowce **19** 25
śnieżna **25** 3
śpioszki **33** 19
śpiwór **89** 26
średnica **79** 12
środek **79** 13
środek do mycia okien **35** 10
środki przekazu **86**
środkowy gracz w polu **93** 2
środkowy osłaniający **93** 27
śruba **37** 38
śrubokręt **37** 24
śrubokręt krzyżakowy **37** 25
świadek **43** 13
światła pozycyjne **51** 49
światło cofania **50** 30
światło odblaskowe **52** 25
światło pozycyjne tylne **50** 31
światło stopu **50** 29
świeczka **29** 27
świnia **67** 30
tabletka **41** 6
tablica **76** 5, **92** 19
tablica narzędziowa **36** 15
tablica ogłoszeń **76** 7
tablica wyników **93** 19
tabliczka (czekolady) **13** 18
taca **16** 33
tacka na kredę **76** 9
taczka **27** 32, **82** 23
taksometr **55** 23
taksówka **55,** **55** 27
taksówkarz **55** 26
talerz **29** 13
talerzyk na chleb z masłem **29** 11
tamburyn **98** 17
tancerz **99** 3
taniec **99**
taras **27** 5
tarcza **65** 18a
taśma **15** 23, **46** 22, **56** 12

taśm izolacyjna **37** 34
tchawica **5** 60
teatr **99**
teczka **21** 37
teczka na akta **83** 22
Teksas **73** 43
telefon **32** 26, **83** 15
telefonistka **83** 1
teleskop **74,** 22
teleskopy **52** 31
telewizor **28** 18, **100** 5
temblak **39** 3
temperatura **25** 6
temperówka **76** 20, **83** 30
tenis **94**
tenis stołowy **94**
tenisówki **20** 11
Tennessee **73** 42
terier **69** 25
termit **63** 11
termofor **41** 4
termometr **25** 5, **78** 22
termos **88** 14
tęczówka **5** 47
tętnica **5** 69
tkanie **101** 30
toga **43** 11
topola **61** 30
toporek **36** 17
topór **42** 14
tor **94** 4, **94** 25, **95** 12, **95** 19
tor golfowy **95**
tor przeszkód **87** 17
tor wyścigowy **95**
torba **15** 25, **66** 4b
torba golfowa **95** 7
torba na listy **46** 4
torba na ramię **21** 35
torba na ubrania **56** 1
torba na zakupy **20** 18
torbacze **66**
torebka **12** 8, **20** 23
tory **54** 10
traktor **81** 15
tramwaj **55** 30

tramwaj linowy **55** 32

transformator **80** 25

trap **58** 20

tratwa **89** 16

tratwa nadmuchiwana **59** 20

trawnik **27** 15, **95** 10

trawy **60**

trąba **66** 17a

trąbka **52** 5, **98** 25

trener **93** 21

trójkąt **79** 6

trójkąt prostokątny **79** 22

trójkołowiec **52** 6

truskawka **8** 15

tryb główny **52** 20

trybunał **43** 16

trybuny **93** 10

trygon **65** 6

trzcina cukrowa **60** 20

trzeć **31** 2

trzecia częsć **79** 32

trzustka **5** 71

trzymać **17** 12

trzymacz do garnków **30** 34

tuba **13** 15, **98** 27

tulipan **60** 1

turyści piesi **88** 2

tusz do oczu **23** 33

tusz do rzęs **23** 28

twarz **4** 1

tygrys **68** 2

tylna klapa **51** 43

tylny zderzak **51** 42

tytuł **47** 9

ubijać **31** 8

ubrania na co dzień **20–21**

ubrania wierzchnie **19**

ucho **4** 34

uchwyt **37** 43b, **54** 8

uczeń **76** 19

uderzać **96** 1

udko **11** 19

udo **4** 18

udziec **10** 14

ukąszenie owada **40** 3

układ słoneczny **74**

układanka **33** 31

ukulele **98** 3

ulica **45** 31

ułamki **79**

umywalka **34** 19

uprzątać **17** 6

uprząż **89** 22

Ural **71** 46

Uran **74** 17

urazy **40**

urząd pocztowy **46**

urzędnik pocztowy **46** 14

usta **4** 2

Utah **73** 44

Vermont **73** 45

w **102** 7

w dół **103** 3

w groszki **24** 19

w kratkę **24** 18

w paski **24** 17

w szkocką kratę **24** 22

waciki **33** 10, **39** 23

waga **14** 7, **34** 32, **78** 4

wagon **54** 9

wagonik **80** 8

wahadłowiec **75** 14

walec **79** 26

walizka **56** 7

walkman firmy Sony **100** 30

wałek **30** 25, **37** 29

wanna **34** 11

warga **4** 43

warsztat **36–37**

warzywa **6–7**

Waszyngton **73** 47

watowanie **101** 32

wazon **28** 6

ważka **63** 4

wąsy **4** 40

wątroba **5** 65

wąż **42** 8, **51** 57

wąż ogrodowy **27** 14

wąż prążkowany **65** 9

wchodzić **77** 14

wejście na pokład **56**

wełna **101** 23

wentyl **52** 27

wentylator sufitowy **28** 1

Wenus **74** 12

wędka **88** 7

wędkarstwo **88**

węgiel **80** 7

węgiel drzewny w brykietach **27** 23

węgorz **65** 4

wiaderko **90** 16

wiadro **35** 15

wiadukt **53** 3

wiatr **80** 4

wiatrak **80** 19

wiatrówka **19** 5

wiąz **61** 36

wiązać **77** 12

wiązanie **95** 16

widelec **29** 12

wideo **100**

widły **81** 14

wielbłąd **67** 33

Wielka Pustynia Piaszczysta **71** 55

wieloryb **68** 9

wieprz **67** 30

wieprzowina **10** 6

wiertarka elektryczna **37** 43

wiertło **37** 43a

wierzba **61** 31

wierzchołek **79** 21

wieszać **38** 6

wieszak **32** 1

wieszak na ręczniki **34** 25

wietrznie **25** 13

wiewiórka **66** 10

wiewiórka ziemna **66** 6

wieża chłodząca **80** 16

wieża kontrolna **57** 20

wieża wiertnicza **80** 2

wieżyczka **48** 12

wilk **69** 29

winda **45** 17, **80** 9

winda kotwiczna **58** 23

windsurfer **59** 14

wino **16** 19

winorośl **61** 42

wiolonczela **98** 9

wiosło **59** 3, **59** 22

wiosna **26**

Wirginia **73** 46

Wirginia Zachodnia **73** 48

Wisconsin **73** 49

wiśnia **9** 19

wjazd **53** 21

wkład do myjki **35** 11

wkład do skoroszytu **76** 13

wkładka do gotowania na parze **30** 3

wkręt **37** 42

właz **45** 32

włącznik **37** 43c

włosy **4** 30

wnuczek **2** 12

wnuczka **2** 11

woda **42** 16, **91** 30

woda do picia **87** 19

wodospad **80** 11, **89** 18

wodze **94** 22

wodzireje **93** 20

wokalistka **99** 24

wołowe mielone **10** 2

wołowina **10** 1

wołowina duszona **18** 14

worek z lodem **41** 4

wóz pożarniczy **42** 2

wózek **15** 19, **56** 6

wózek dziecięcy **45** 27

wózek golfowy **95** 8

wózek spacerowy **33** 14

wózek ręczny **87** 4

wózek widłowy **58** 4

wróbel **64** 10

wrzut listów **46** 13

wschód **71** 73

wskaźnik poziomu paliwa **50** 9

wspinaczka wysokogórska **89**

wszechświat **74**

wtyczka **32** 26b, **37** 43d

wtyczka z uziemieniem **36** 7

wuj **3** 3

wychodzić **77** 13

wyciąg narciarski **95** 18

wycieraczka **50** 6

wycierać (do sucha) **38** 9

wycierać na mokro **38** 5

wycinarka **36** 3

wydmy **90** 12

wydra **68** 10

wydruk **83** 8

wykładzina **28** 15

wykrój **101** 6

wykrywacz dymu **33** 15

wykrywacz metali **56** 10

wymiary **79**

Wyoming **73** 50

wypieki **14** 11

wyposażenie **89** 27

wypożyczalnia **47** 2

wyrzutnia **75** 15

wysięgnik z gondolą **82** 18

wysoki **24** 11

wysoki obcas **20** 25

wysokie buty nieprzemakalne **88** 10

wysokie ciśnienie **40** 10

wysokie krzesło **16** 8

wysokość **79** 34

wysypka **40** 1

wyścigi konne **94**

wytwarzanie energii **80**

wywrotka **49** 14

wzgórza **88** 4

wzorzysty **24** 21

yam **7** 24

z **103** 7, **103** 10

za **102** 9

zachód **71** 74

zacisk **78** 7

zaćmienie Księżyca **74** 6

zaćmienie Słońca **75** 10

zagłówek **50** 35

zagon **81** 18

zagroda **81** 24

zajęcia na świeżym powietrzu **88–89**

zakraplacz **78** 26

załoga **75** 12

zamarzanie **25** 11

zamawiać **17** 5

zamek z piasku **91** 32

zamek błyskawiczny **101** 16

zamiatać **38** 7

zamiatarka uliczna **49** 1

zamknąć **77** 5

zamknięty **24** 16

zamrażarka **14** 3, **30** 20

zapalać **17** 13

zapałki (w książeczce) **16** 28

zapalniczka **16** 30

zapiekana fasola **18** 3

zapięcie **23** 17

zapora **80** 18, **82** 21

zasłona **32** 10, **34** 5

zasłony **28** 23

zastawa **29** 1

zastrzyk **41** 8

zasypka **33** 7

Zatoka Alaska **70** 17

Zatoka Bengalska **70** 32

Zatoka Gwinejska **70** 25

Zatoka Hudsona **70** 18

Zatoka Meksykańska **70** 19

Zatoka Perska **70** 28

zatoki **70**

zatrzask **23** 19, **101** 13

zawodnik chwytający **92** 2

zawodnik grający w golfa **94** 10

zawodnik małej ligi **92** 8

zawodnik miotający **93** 12

zawodnik odbijający **92** 7, **93** 14

zawody **84–86**

ząb **4** 42

ząbek **7** 25a

zbiornik paliwa **50** 34

zbiornikowiec **58** 15

zbocze narciarskie **95**

zboża **60**

zderzak przedni **51** 51

zdrapywać **26** 15

zebra **66** 18

zegar **76** 2

zegarek **23** 10

zestaw do preparowania **78** 33

zestaw sześciu puszek **13** 13

zestaw stereofoniczny **28** 20

zestaw wykrojów **101** 7

zielony groszek **6** 17

Ziemia **74** 8, **74** 13

ziemniak **7** 23

zima **26**

zimno **25** 10

zioła **6** 9

zjazd **53** 2

zjeżdżalnia **87** 12

zlewka **78** 23

złamana kość **40** 15

zmazać **77** 3

zmieniać (pościel) **38** 13

zmywacz **76** 11

zmywarka do naczyń **30** 1

znaczek pocztowy **46** 10

znak drogowy **44** 8, **53** 23

znak ograniczenia szybkości **53** 8

znak zjazdu **53** 24

zoo **87** 1

zrywać **26** 7

zszywacz **83** 27

zwichnięcie **40** 13

zwierzęta proste **62**

zwierzyna płowa **67** 26

żaba **65** 17

żagiel **59** 9

żaglówka **59** 4

żakiet **21** 33

żaluzje **32** 12

żarówka **35** 22

żądło **63** 8a

żeberka **10** 10

żelazko **35** 12

żołądek **5** 66

żołądź **61** 33b

żołnierz **48** 16

żołnierz piechoty morskiej **48** 18

żona **2** 4

żonkil **60** 8

żółty narcyz **60** 8

żółw **65** 18

żółw morski **65** 12

żuk **63** 10

żurawina **8** 13

żyła **5** 68

żyletki **23** 23

żyłka **88** 8

żyrafa **67** 29

żyrandol **29** 3

źrebię **67** 22

źrenica **5** 48

źródełko **87** 19

źródła energii **80**